BURNING CROWN GLORY

Chronicle 25

Panagiota Makaronis

KREA PREA (TM). Est. 2012

Copyright © October 2025 Panagiota Makaronis

All rights reserved

The characters and events portrayed in this book are fictitious. Any similarity to real persons, living or dead, is coincidental and not intended by the author.

No part of this book may be reproduced, or stored in a retrieval system, or transmitted in any form or by any means, electronic, mechanical, photocopying, recording, or otherwise, without express written permission of the publisher.

ISBN: 978-1-7641457-6-3

Cover design by: Copilot Panagiota Makaronis
Written in Australia, Victoria, Melbourne, Craigieburn
Editor: KREA PREA (TM). Est. 2012

I dedicate this book to those who hit run & assume the outcome will help them rise. There is no challenge here, I have out done you, I hit my mark.
Good-bye
X

Those who have departed; a life, less lived, just to please those who create the piece. Never truly lived, nor did they truly leave, the belief system took over the need. Its Spirit lingers, while its soul remains searching for answers.

Unruly & unfinished business.

So, wanting to clear a debt, before they cross over.

A silent Oath written in Heaven, Casting a spell in Hell. Just to hand the next generation, an energy. That will immerse in eternal bliss to some, or to others Eternal damnation. To he who returned to steal another key.

Time moves, fast; forced and furious. Facing, reasonable doubt, forwarding towards a drive to the other side. All while attempting to integrate with those who elevate with ease.

Stepping into a trace, that will hand them peace. A path, less travelled; when they see the light.

Safe Travels!

PANAGIOTA MAKARONIS

CONTENTS

Title Page
Copyright
Dedication
Epigraph
INTRODUCTION 1
CHAPTER 1 4
CHAPTER 2 14
CHAPTER 3 27
CHAPTER 4 40
CHAPTER 5 53
CHAPTER 6 66
CHAPTER 7 79
CHAPTER 8 92
CHAPTER 9 105
CHAPTER 10 118
About The Author 133
The Theatrical Melodia of my Life Chronicle 1 137

Books By This Author

INTRODUCTION

Burning Crown of Glory; Chronicle 25. The continuation of my Memoirs.

I found myself in a position of questioning the motives of certain individuals. I was put in a situation, that had me forced to override, run hide, and return when needed. The clock was ticking, and those who were relentless and ruthless were scheming. I could not fight back, I felt I was ganged up on.

It got to the point I did not know who was in on it and where to turn. Way too many tricks, all I knew, it pushed me in the corner; towards paranoia and that is what got me through. The deceit raised an alarm. A lack of empathy had come my way, and I could not retrieve another damn day.

All I knew is, I was bombarded by the lie; to hand the corrupt truth. Just to give the unjust, credibility in an impromptu evaluation. Creating an image that ended in a fake and false reality. In the end I could not have cared less, I found my common ground and my journey continued nevertheless.

Even though I went through a blow, I had to heal and continue on my journey; revealing the truth. I found myself in a position of blocking certain individuals from my peripheral vision. Just to find those who were misguided detaching them. The notion attaching to my etheric chord will hand them truth.

For those who joined to me, on the purpose of confusing my reality. Were about to be hit with a hold up. Grieving over a loved one was their outcome, mine was healing from a fall, one I hope I rise above and beyond. Look back at it a lesson lived; a learning curve a strengthening mechanism.

Anything to keep me from losing another sense of reality. I was certain I was working in unison with my body and soul, holding on to the finals; a second trial. As I continued to process my progress, wired, I gave up; stating a fact. It gave me a chance to catch up and catch the corrupt in advance.

All while the corrupt confessed, paying out parts of a debt. For those who were working under the raider, were to push me off track. It became a reality kick, to a game that had been pending. It had come to my attention that I was being stalked; by those who carried a dull torch.

For what reason, I could not state a fact, because I had no proof. I was being attacked, pushed off the edge. Whatever I did the world was large and the attacks were absolutely childish. It was all a bluff, to throw me a bone so I waste time; chewing while I was brewing over it.

All I knew I was not wrong all along. Trying to get out, was rubbing several individuals the wrong way. For that reason, I lost my intense faith in Humanity. What I did to deserve such a serve, only they knew. I strongly believed it was part expectation I could not meet.

It was an issue that reinforced, and had me hit back with remorse. It left me stepping into the unknown, on my own accord. Releasing what I thought will come to an end; that is when I knew the corrupt hit a dead-end. When I entered that trace, it brought me praise.

Trapping me with a curse that will serve me well. Presenting the corrupt with an upcoming spell. For the goal that had me working in unison with a challenge, started with a Big Bang. A theory that had me raise the buck. It caused an effect and brought me forward; a brand-new thread.

A trace that warned me I was way too hard on myself. There was no reason for me to feed off that treason. For those who had me locked in for their own safety are now Grieving. Lost and forgotten because I gave in gave it my best shot. I was long gone here; I completed my task regardless. I was under a spell, that left me to dwell in hell. A world that handed me the energy I needed to continue.

"TWO-UP CORRUPT ALL BETS ARE ON! HEADS OR TAILS?"

CHAPTER 1

◆ ◆ ◆

THE DANGERS WE FACE WHEN OUR SOCIAL CIRCLE TURNS CORRUPT

I was torn in more than direction; it forced to remain silent, trapped in the middle of a diversion. I was lead on, left to preach my truth on my own. Several, saw my potential and could not wait to push me off the edge so I never pledge. Lucky for me I took it as a strength to power through.

I was handed redemption, from that rejection. Hitting the corrupt at every validation. Because those who were part of that circle, created a trace it led me to return repeat and replace. All while those who knew were covering up one more clue. It gave me a chance to release that beast.

Warned I hit the end of that lease, wording it in a way that led me astray. Where the corrupt were returning to betray me with the same old dilemma. Assuming making me there victim again will hand them a key; from victim to victory. It left me focused on the old starting new.

Thinking that the dream will create a challenge in-between. It served me a presentation that caved I on me when I hit the end of that reservation. It gave me trace; it served me well it handed me a given trend that took me on a journey bound to fail again.

If I did not tread carefully, the trace will become erratic and I will fall into a systematic approach. It freed me from that trend that traced me in the end. It forced me to redo and reclaim a true rude awakening, in the end of the race. I was left to repeat replace and reclaim a division to the game.

A given approach that served me well, forced me to hit back and face another trend in the end of that spell. The troubles I face took me on a journey that forced me to reclaim another trace to that case. It had me facing the end of the race with the notion I hit the end of that erosion cleansed.

In fact, it created a trace, where the end of the race, will retrace my upcoming event. I had to release and feed off the beast. Where I get in finalize that win and case close that trend that had me repeating another dead-end. I was to return, for one more entrance to the unknown.

It led me to decide what trace will override the past, and

what will create a diversion to that request. Just to help me survive another test. In the end I was left to portray another bad day. It had me face a case that caused an effect and fed off that trend that had me repeating a death-threat.

A trace that left me presenting the corrupt with another request, had me blind sighted. For what I thought was the truth, lined me up for one more chance to hit the corrupt in advance. In fact, it had me deep in thought, trying to repeat what I thought was the last resort.

In fact, it was part of a trace that had me forced to give in. It had me face another case; it caused an effect and prepared me for another trend. Hoping the corrupt hit a dead end and the only way in was to win my trust. But my interest had changed, my space rearranged, and credentials released.

For that reason, the corrupt were getting angrier. Trapping, by tracking me down and tricking me into an oblivion. Assuming failing me will hand them a fight and a new key. Because I fell, they lost a fight and the only way to get back on track was to catch up and create another trace to that case.

Meanwhile we wait, while I heal, so the corrupt can continue to ride the wave, to the end of that trend. It was causing effects, making me see I was hitting a divine energy. It had me trapping he who knew and creating a war in the peace of he who warned me he had a clue.

because he who knew had him locked in, forcing me to

hit back and win. I had to follow up on another trace. It was handing me the invasion I needed to reclaim and follow up on another game.

For the only way they could get back on track was present me with a key. For the only thing I needed to get in and finalize that win was trace, trap and create a trend. It handed me a trial error and a brand-new drama. Even then the corrupt turned against me, they took me in and fed off me.

It was trapping my every movement. Just to catch a moment, face my fear and clear the air, all while I catch up and free myself from another scare. Skipping he who knew, was causing the effects I needed to cast a spell and reap a reward, by trapping he who had a clue.

Forcing him to cave in on the concept, breaking the silence was undoubtable. I was taught a lesson and left to heal. I was to trap that lead that lined me up for a case. Put on a journey that had me replace what I thought was my last chance; before I got in and rose above that inning.

I gave it my best shot; I had to uncover a lead and undo that feed. So, when the time come ride that wave, that was to save me. It took me under, led me towards a path that had me no longer wonder. I was handed the power to undo and devour while I unfold another case.

Create a war in the peace of those who take and not give. Purely for their own selfish woes. Just to treat he who knew with a trail an error and bribe him with terror. With a final degree on my side, the only thing that had me override was the last chance to cancel the corrupt out in advance.

It was trapping he who forced me to release the beast. So, when I catch them in the act, the trace becomes a case and the trend becomes, unworthy in the end. All so I can find peace, finalize that drama, a case, that caused an effect and presented me with a trial an error; a final vendetta.

Handing me the entitlement to hit, then kick back and watch the corrupt erupt. It was harming me, knowing I was in, but had no entrance to win. Because my freedom was cut short by, he who knew working in unison with he who had a clue. Neither of them could embrace that case.

Because I was handed a trial an error; a test that broke the cycle. For he who knew created a presentation that formed an investigation. Trapping me every final minor manifestation. It harmed me while I caught up, it trapped me, while the system stalled and presented with a long haul.

It was long enough to give me a kick start, not hard enough to feed off the concept. It left me stagnant beyond my disbelief, where I staled just to witness the longer, I stalled the less likely I was to see the light. There was a demon in my vicinity ready and willing to fight.

Little did I know, that the little demon was my perception; not my protection. It was a little white lie created by the corrupts deception to keep me guessing wrong; so, they can remain strong. The conditions to my mission, were set up and I was set alight, by he who knew.

He was causing effects, with he who had a clue. It created structural of events, that had me forced to fail. then fall. Meanwhile I attempt to fight back and resurrect from that defeat. For the energy that was unworthy entered my realm and left me forced to repeat return and finalize that debt.

It was handing me a brand-new threat, a challenge that made me see, I was a victim of scrutiny. It had come to my attention; someone had entered my realm with an enticed energy. Inconsistent to what was true. It did not make sense, on what I had to do, to kindly state a fact.

Because I was too busy trying to get back on track. The energy that that served me well then heard my call now. It gave me a trace that served me well. It handed me an opportunity to stand tall and feed off the trend. It was breaking my silence and attempting to harm me again.

All while I caught up and forced the corrupt to return an finalize that test that had me facing another trace. A past test that was on the mend had closed and the case was too easy to erase. It had taught me a valuable lesson and that was to create an acute faith, a trace less likely for me to lose.

It was part of a trend that had me repeating, I on the edge of deleting a trend. It had me attempt the worse so

I can reverse, hitting back with one more verse. Because the corrupt were attempting to harm me right in the middle of a trace, it had me trapped in the end of the race.

I was not aware that I had several naysayers, working in unison. Devaluing me and my energy, attempting to coverup another trend. Assuming that the power was still theirs and I gave in. In fact, I was prewarned, hit back with a curse I could reverse, and a trace that hit me when I hit the end.

That verse was part of a curse that was pending, it was a trace that was never ending. The corrupt had overdone that plan and left me forced to hit back with remorse. Which made things worse not only they hit me way below the belt but I was stuck. I could not fight back and I felt isolated.

I was left stranded wondering what the hell I did do to deserve such a failed outcome. They were once again, working under the raider planning to harm me again. I on the other end feeling the pressure, waiting for the next hit. Praying to God it backfires and I win.

Because I thought it was finished, the troubles were intense. I had way too many mood-swings; I could not sense a positive outcome. I was set free to do what I set out to do. But they bred a new breed, assuming that will harm me and leave facing another harsh reality.

In fact, it had me face an uncertainty; likely to question humanity holistically. Where I was charmed beyond repair, and the only thing I had left to look forward to what I created when I was on the move repeating a new statement. It was part of a trace that forced me to redo a new review.

Catch up, all while I feed of the corrupt, then return for one more hassle a haste to terrorize the corrupts method at the end of that trace. It had me face another case, a failed faith, a test where the patience of those who hit me and ran run thin. All while it runs its course and hand me a win.

I had to repeat, leave it to chance, for the choice I made left me hunting for more. It had me reassured that the trace was no longer a bet. But a tread, of violence to stir the pot and give me the impression that the trace was accompanied by creative sense a restyle that haunted me at the end.

Seen as an easy target, had me forced to repeat, so I can catch up. For what it was worth, the journey had to go through that cause of action. For the trace handed me a case. It had me face an ending that was pending. Where I was on the edge personally attacking those who purge.

All so I can return and curse he who harmed me. For it was he who held me back, he took me in fed off me from within. Challenged me in a fight, so when I reached my pinnacle, the trace remained pending and the trap, forced me to redo; became part of a silent treatment.

It had the corrupt surrender, pushing me in the corner. It left me suffering so they can continue to hit back and revitalize a trace to that case. It caused an effect and presented me with a defect. A step into a wrong direction, straight into a follow up on a given reward.

It stated a fact, challenging the corrupt so I can hit back. It had me feeding off the impact. It had me facing another step into a direction that had me failing a resurrection. All while I was on the path of making it happen. All I had to do was uncover up another review feed off the concept.

While I trap those who coincide with the truth. It had me finalizing that method so I can return and hit back with a trace that stalled. I was stalked by those who were taught, how to tail and take the bait. Allegedly would make a difference, line me up with a curse, that had me return with a verse.

All it did was have me return and hand them a taste of their own filth. It was to restore my energy and face the facts. It created a contact, that purely took me in. Face my demon, and hand me the motivation to write a wrong. While feeding off the corrupt; so, I can remain strong.

For what I thought was a trap, was a mistake that pushed me off track. It had me catch up clear the debt. Forced to get in release that demon from within. I was to catch up face the facts, feed off the trace, terrorize those energies that took me in. It had me feed off the drama that belted me; within.

A follow up on a trace fed off the trend and broke the silence in the end. Instead of giving in, it gave me the power to induce that truce. I was to entrap that test that took me on the wrong path. I had to divide and conquer while I devour. For the corrupt saw me as an easy target.

A chance to salvage whatever dignity I had left had pushed me in the corner. It produced a trace that had me facing a case. Because I was belted way too many times it took me on a path that had me reserved for another a case. It had me face a clear return that took me in and fed of the ending.

It had me causing an effect breaking the silence so I can reset. All because the energy that had me face a fear case closed. It caused an effect and released that demon that lined me up for another reason. Just to hit back with treason, a trace that had me failing that test.

CHAPTER 2

◆ ◆ ◆

TIME TO RELEASE THAT BEAST & SHOCK THE SYSTEM

I was to repeat, test the corrupts patience and press delete. For what happened back when, was not just a test of endurance; it was a dead end. It was to push me in the corner, so I continue to pretend. Delete delay and purely start again; trapped in the middle of a damn scam; a theme in between.

Where this time around, I stopped pretending and started reminiscing. It caused an effect, trapped the corrupt in the middle of that threat. So, I can clear the deck, for a new thrill then prepare myself for a treat that served me well and forced me to hit back; while going through hell.

It restored my energy and faced me; right before I was hit back with an encore. The action had led me to an abreaction, that had restored my energy. It gave me a second chance, to get back on track and feed off the impact. It was part of a trend that hit me with a blow, forcing the corrupt to undo.

I had to follow up on another review, with a passionate view. It was part of a case I could close, then follow up on a test. So, when I reach my pinnacle I could convince, bear the pain while I push the corrupt in the corner and press replay. Then when they least expect it, cover up; feed off the trace.

It was part of a dead end; it led me towards a journey that forced me to regain conscious awareness again. It had me repeat, report, and cover up a chance in advance. Then alleviate, what I thought was part of the last resort. Bighting my tongue, long enough to see the corrupt wrap it all up.

A challenge that saw me easy, caused way too many effects. It had messed up my head, trying to get ahead. I was fighting a lost cause writing a wrong trying my hardest to remain strong. For I was on the move feeding off the terror that had me facing another error.

I had to repeat, get back on track, and delete; whatever held me back. Only to witness the challenge was ravaged and I could not salvage a thing. The trace was a joke and the trend in the end had me facing another dead end. I was hit with every trial chased at every vile handed denial.

Where every bend set me back, trapping those who pushed me of track. For that served me wrong I could erase a thing unless I handed the corrupt another chance to win. If only I could return and hit the corrupt with one more case. It challenged me with a task that presented me with a gift.

A foundation to harm the corrupt at every resurrection was manifesting. For I was mend feeding off the trace that had me prepared for a dead end. Just before the case closed, I was given an ultimatum. Where I rose above and beyond hitting an ending that was pending.

It was part of a trace, that trapped me in the middle of a chaos. Stating a fact, had case closed that trend, preparing me for a new practice. It served me well in the end of that silent rivalry that handed me poison ivy. It led me towards a journey that handed me a dead-end.

Stating a fact, had me trapping those who were intact. They were playing the game, as if they had power to gamble and prepare me for another shame. A scam and a scheme that backfired in between, had me restoring my energy and handing me a brand-new spanking clue.

A curse I could reverse, waited for me to return with the same old seed. The one that was planted before I could breathe. A challenge that forced me to reveal, had me face my fear. For the corrupts final feast, reserved me the right to accomplish another fight.

It served me well and presented me with a trap. I was handed a key to help me get back on track. It led me to fight back. All because I was trying to let go while the corrupt were attaching to my spirit. so, they can return hit back and harm me so I never voice my opinion.

Leaving me doubting myself was one way. Eventually I will get through that too, rise above and beyond and force my way up, teaching the corrupt a valuable lesson. I had to claim and hit the corrupt back with the same game. It was hitting me every time I was handed a way out.

Assuming the trace was part of a final case. It turned me upside-down; it fed off me when I hit the end of the race. I was handed a trial that had me challenge. It took me in and validated another win. A moment to realize the only thing that had me warned from within was the outcome.

Entering, and witness a prior inning. A presentation that was meant to be for another, had taught me how to praise and follow up on a game. Every time I hit the end I failed to attend. It was tormenting me, applying for that trace was accompanied by my spirit; entering a better place.

All so I can release that feast, that had me skip a beat. Because I forced my way through, I failed in the end. I could not trust a living soul, no one cared I was stuck trying to get through while everyone around me ignored my calls for help. It left me struggling heaved waiting to be saved.

For he who knew me, wanted to screw me right through. He took me in and fed off me from within. I was nowhere to be found; I had no freedom to go around. I could not fix a thing that damage that forced me to recreate another trace to that case, served me well from within.

It gave me a second chance to break the corrupts cycle. I had Pushed them in the corner and fed off their existence with admiration and persistence. Just so I can catch up catch a break the cycle. I had to finalize the energy that forced me to repeat, replace, feed off the trial; hand the corrupt terror.

An error that had me hit back with pleasure. Because they locked me in and left me facing another dead end in the end. I was left to repeat trap those who delete delay he who went down this path assuming he had the power to embark and follow up on another review.

Every time I tried to find a way out and get back on track. I would be stuck in the same damn train of thought. Left to suffer so the corrupt can prosper. Where I had to handle it with care. A task where I had to face a glum future. No freedom just a solid foundation with a few cracks that needed repair.

It forced me to erase that trace that held me back. It had me finalizing the case that served me well in the end. A trend at the end of the race, that warned me I was about to hit a threat that had me facing another debt. A given opportunity for me to aggravate; what the corrupt established.

When I am to rise above that fall, the fight to get me through will help me face another day. It will bring forth light, lit by the Gods of the night. Where at the end of the tunnel, I will find my way through, handing the corrupt a challenge where they hold on to that final review.

Testing each other's patience so I can get through. Was part of my creativity that had me humble ready to fight back and face a trace at the end of the race. I was taught a lesson left to release that feast so when I caught up, I could repeat repel and restart that trend that put me through hell.

It had me facing a detection to that manifestation. It was part of a defect, where that demon who was stalking me had warned others to back down so he can get a crack at it. He made himself easy prey to me; he now became my victim and I got to play the demon.

He made himself an enemy, trying to get in and feed off me. But in the end, I fell and rose; not as quick as I hoped. But each strength had given me the power to ache within and devour. But then again, time heals all wounds. Each wound had a nasty cut, each time I tried to heal it had opened.

Yet again I kept trying to seal it. Waiting for the trace to erase and the trend to incorporate another final in the end. It was causing effect and hitting a lead to that line up that faced me when I least expected it. So, when the trend became a huge burden in the end I left to start anew.

Where in the end what was to come my way, had me pressing replay. Following up on a bad day. I had to condition the mission and follow up on another competition. It was part of a trend that was stirring the pot. Lining me up for one more chance to cast a spell; while the corrupt failed and fell.

In the beginning I was to line up the trace that fed off the case. It had me cancel out the end of that trend. Bring forth peace to what I thought would become the last resort. Where the freedom, I needed to succeed, had me alarmed at the end of that trend; where I had to start again.

All so I can claim my thoughts, alleviate, try not to aggravate those who knew. Finalize the outcome so I can catch up; breaking the siren. It gave the corrupt a chance to catch a break. It harmed me in the end and the trend saw me as an easy target; Trapping the corrupt in the end of that market.

I had to follow up on a review and feed off the concept so can skip that too. For taking the intuitive and following up on a backup. would bring me forth. It would not be hard to astound those who were using me to get in. Because every time I hit the punch line; a second trial will serve me denial.

It would cave in on the concept, give me a chance to reap a reward. I was to set a precedent get back on track present the corrupt with a trick. Just to cancel out what I thought was part of a threat. Hit in the end of that debt, with a trace that will form an alliance.

Handing me a second chance to break the silence. Only to witness I hit the end of that trend with a curse I could reverse. I had to release that demon that pushed me out of place. I had to sweeten the deal and hand out what I thought was doubt. In fact, it was part of a trace that led me to repeat.

I had to replace and follow up on another key. just so I can catch up and feed of the corrupts anomaly. In fact, it was part of a trace that trapped me in the end of the race. It was forcing me to reclaim what I thought was the last resort and the beginning of a new inning.

I had to divide, conquer, follow up on a game. Just so I can catch the corrupt right before they were about to hit me again. Where this time the trace became my finally. Catching them in the act of betrayal was a vile sail. A vicious cycle, once over; where they caused effect and handed me a test.

When I was working on a good cause, the trace becomes part of a restoration to that manifestation. A resemblance to a trend that caused an effect and gave me a chance to hit back and advance. Where I had to attend a good cause trapping those who hit back with remorse.

Where every time I hit an ending, a challenge will serve me right. It helped me follow up on another fight. A burning sensation that handed me an ending that will bring forth peace. Caused the effects I needed to claim another trace at the end of the game. For I had no time to release that feast.

It was my chance to catch up, test those who used me to get there. Then when the trace had me leading the pact, it served me well and presented me with a key that forced me to release that demon that gave me a chance to finalize that test that had me regress.

I had no trend to get back on track. What I had was a feast, it taught me a lesson. It had me reach that trend that led me towards a journey that taught me well in the end. Because I was on the edge, trying to get back a key note a challenge that took me on a pathway that led me astray.

For what was stolen, had me on the wrong path. I had to force my way through, waiting to face another case. For what was to come from that trend led me to believe I hit an ending that was pending. It had me forced to hit back with remorse.

I had to feed off the impact and start fresh. Case those who were serving me wrong so when I caught up, I could hit back and remain strong. For the method took me on a passageway that lined me for a wrong turn. Led me to release and bribe the corrupt so I can find peace.

In the end, they needed me again, and I was on the cusp of finalizing everything. I had to catch up and finalize that trace. I was too busy following up on a method that was haunting me. I missed the boat, yet again, I faced another trend creating a foundation to pretend.

It had me forced to hit back with remorse. I was given a foundation that served me a reservation. It caused an effect and broke me when I hit the end of that reservation. There was no warning, because I hit a yearning. In the end I was not aware that the corrupt were on the move.

It had me trapping he who knew, and he who had a clue. Warning everyone to stand clear, because he was planning another hit. Only to witness the trace was based on a case, that was part of a given and a trick that was forbidden. So, when the time come, I could return and belt the corrupt.

The only time I was served well was when I was handed a forthcoming spell. For the key that restored my energy landed me a role. So, when I hit the end there was no foundation just a final restoration. It was part of an entrance that gave me a free-ride to the other side.

It was the last thing that took me in and raided my head from within. Where I was taught a lesson and given an opportunity to finalist and feed off the extended warranty. Even then I had no freedom to win, where every lease fed off my piece. Cornered, so I can release that beast.

I had to get through finalize that energy that had me on the move. I was returning for one chance to hit back in advance. I had to feed off the energy that served me a first and final priority. Then when the time come reserve the right for the corrupt to return and fight back with a wasted outcome.

Because I had no choice but to feed off the challenge I was served. The chance I was given had me finally on the move trapped in the middle of a final test. It was harming me, because I had no freedom to give in. Because every time I was heading for a fall, I had to return and rise above it all.

It had me reaping a reward and creating a faith that had me warned once again. For that chance of a life time, created a piece, it forced me to release and trace that case that caused an effect. It brought me forward so I can resurrect. It was all a lie, purely to have me fight for my life.

I had to retrain my thoughts, and force my way in. It gave me the passion and the power to win. All so I can get in and retrieve everything, that was taken from me when I was pushed off the edge. For those who used me to get in, assumed harming me will give them the power to win.

I had to force my way through, and raise awareness. Then when the time come face my fear and finalize that trend that had me repeat and start again. Every outcome had me undo another review. It gave me a chance to hit back in advance, so when I reached my peak; I could redo start new.

I was on the mend, stating what I knew was the last review. I had to start again, as if the journey had me release another feast. I had to face my fear and recreate a challenge that will state the facts. It had me back on track creating an anomaly so I rise and change my track of thought.

On the intention I win every redemption. I had to find peace, after that loss, for I was given a challenge and the only way I could undo. I was forced to get in and feed off the trauma that served me well from within. Where I was grief stricken, trying to fight back another trend.

All so I can get back on track and face a new trace in the end. It was part of a hell raising experience, that took me on a journey, that had me on the mend. I was healing from that ordeal where my spirit took over; so, I can finalize that trace earlier. Give in, replace, and make sure I do not lose my place.

It served me well at the end of the race, it had me face my fear while I caught up. I was to release cause an effect, plant a seed, and feed off the corrupt so I can succeed. I was being targeted by a fan, a false friend who was trying to get in and build a follow up from within.

I had to catch them in the act before I fell into a trace. Then erase that case and make sure they no longer pitch in and feed off the trace from within. For that individual who was stalking me from another continent was about to get hit hard. Lose a fight hand me there key and break the silence.

Just so I can walk in freely, not forcefully, there was no need. For every time I hit the end the trace, it became imputable. Long overdue; it was inevitable. I fell into a trial an error repeating a key note just so I can catch up and break that hint of madness; it took me in and harmed me from within.

I had to repeat, for what they did to me was uncanny. Not only they brought me forward but every time I caved in on the journey I would be declined. Defending my honor, and leaving me sacrificing another trace to that spade. It had me forced to return and belt the corrupt with remorse.

CHAPTER 3

♦ ♦ ♦

WHO KNEW? WAS IT YOU?

The end of that passageway became heresy, not only I was left forced to trace that trap. But I was given a reason to cancel out the corrupts treason. It forced my way in and failed the corrupts method from within heaving at the concept while I caught up and faced another failed attempt.

Not only I lost my way but the corrupt challenged me all the way. It had me face my fear, test my patience; repeated another trend. Then when the time come feed off the concept so the corrupt can win another inning in the long run. It created a challenge to get back on track.

It was part of a winning streak that had me free riding; stepping into unknown territory. Where I get in strike back, feed off the impact create an extension to that redemption, then feed of the energy that had me forced to cut back. It had me face another trace, release that beast.

Entertain myself with a new lease, so when the time come undo that clue. For the energy that stated the facts created a piece. It forced me to release and finalize that feast. It had me breaking up with those who faced me, raided my head, and decided to harm me, with a curse I can reverse.

All so I never get there so when I reached my peak, I start again. Waiting for the outcome to rely on me to get by for every trace had a challenge every treat created a piece so when I reached the end of that trend the only case left was the one that had me reach my pinnacle and start again.

For the choice that come my way, created a challenge that will serve me well at the end of the day. when I hit the end of that forthcoming spell the journey that forced me through took me on a journey that had me fail every clue. The trace was to bring forth peace, and present me with a trend.

Breaking the silence, had finalized the ending. The wait was over and the case was trapping me in the middle, trying my luck to cancel out what I thought was part of a curse I could reverse. But it was part of a challenge, that will help me come first. I had to state a fact, start fresh, and try my luck.

When the time come overcome an outcome. In the end there was no trust the trace was canceled and the keys returned to me. But I had no use for them, I fell, injured, healing process took time. The corrupt knew, and cheated, by leaving me stranded. Attempting to steal back those keys.

Where I got to see it, all unfold and everything that come my way had me forced to return and press replay. It had me troubling my spirit. I could not fight back; I was wounded in combat. I lost a fight had to heal and get back up. Because the healing process took its time, I was left suffering in silence

It had me feed off the impact, trapping my soul. It was creating an anomaly in the end of that road. It had me trending in the end, and the only way I could undo was report that theme that was creating a journey that will hand me a clean way out in-between.

It had me reach out to those who hit me and ran. I took the initiative all while hoping the outcome will create a piece; that will bring me forth. Lead those who knew towards a passageway that will give me the energy restore what I had mistaken for. It had me on the edge of recreating a pledge.

It was to lead me onwards, towards a destination that will hand me a key. A challenge that warned me the road to recovery was not as easy as I assumed. I felt the trace take over, the lie underlying a truth. I had to undo, warning me the only troubles that had me release; had me stabilized for peace.

For that feast was the way out, not the way in. I was given a reason to trace trap, hand the corrupt a trial so

I never lose and end living in denial. I ended up reaping a reward at my accord. For the trace had me trapped in the middle of a forthcoming riddle. I had no freedom to release that demon.

In the end I was used and abused again and my foundation was left to my imagination. I was consumed with doubt, handed a confession by those who saw me as an easy target. The freedom I needed to reveal that trace was embraced. It handed me the diversion to replace a trial to that vile.

It had me living in denial, the rejection took over the redemption. It handed me a whole lot of failed attempts. For, everyone who knew wanted more from me and I could not offer a thing; so, they stalked me. Assuming that will bring them joy; all it did was torment the whole concept.

They got in and rejoiced with whomever to haunt me. It became part of a condition that had led me living in repetition where they created a petition to undo and devalue that review. It had created a competition that warned me I had no admission. For what I had was a trace that led me to replay.

I had to regain conscious awareness with mobility to that stability. I had to repeat and remain stable to a game that was gambling that true meaning away. A trace that served me a trend, gave me the power and the energy to pretend. It forced me to redo and follow up on a review.

Just so I can kindly state a fact, catch up and resurrect.

Feed off the concept that had me repeat. The least expected, was part of the trace that had me replace a case. I had to tread lightly before I hit the corrupt spitefully. Press delete delay then let the corrupt in as I catch up and feed off the win.

For winning me over after the fact was a waste it had me face another trace. It caused an effect handed me a dead end to that trend. It had me repeating a new faith, because they hit me and ran and left me troubled again. It started a contest that ended worse before it got better.

That is when I knew I hit a final vendetta. Because I did not give in, they became hostile and I became resentful. The privilege I had undone, it became untrue and I was left suffering right through. I had to undo and repeat, while I recreate another review.

For what they tried to achieve and cause a delay. It had the corrupt on the edge pressing replay. I was asking for a trial and error to be replaced with a presentation that was real. But the corrupt saw me as a threat, after the fact and decided to harm me instead; just to get back on track.

It was troubling me, because I was not interested; the lead turned into a failed reap. I was led on and it had me recreating unprecedented event. Those who were recruited were troubling me I had no freedom or foundation to hit back because I was locked in waiting to get out; from that interest.

It started a fight and brought me forward in the end. It held me up, longing to face another dead end. It was enough for the corrupt to cause an effect, break the silence and resurrect. I was truly praised for a trend that will end in tragedy. For I was given a trace that served me well either way.

I decided to set it free and pray to God the corrupt fall fail, losing their pride. Because they were laid to rest, before they had a chance to process. I was given a chance to hit back in advance. The trace that had me face a case, warned me the energy I once carried led me towards scrutiny.

It was heaving at me, and every threat took me on a pathway that had me stagnant to my development. I was issued a faith less likely for me to release, peace. I was given a presentation that had me returning for another investigation. Yearning for a way out, even tried to reclaim a game.

Only to witness the end of that trend was harming me, so I never win another inning. For that feast forced me to undo and follow upon another review. For every time I was given a challenge, I was served with a trace. It had me replace another case. Then repeat a journey that had me on the edge.

I had to finalize that trace, press delete while I take the initiative and fall into a lie. I gave me the power to get in and feed off the trace that failed me at the end of the race. I was taught a lesson left to invade in the corrupts privacy, just so I can catch up and feed off the trace that had me repeat.

I had to replace, what I thought it was part of a given.

In fact, I had to start fresh, a vile attempt that had me facing another temp. A trace to that case, that forced me to replace that final review. I had no time to undo nor follow up on a trend; for it had me facing a terrible act of kindness.

Where I was given a trace that had me facing a day to press replay. A common report to serve me well gave me a test to put the corrupt through hell. This time around I was served well, it had me facing a forthcoming spell. While I was going through the motions, the test had me on the edge.

In the end I had to erase my pain, reverse the curse; claim the game. Handing the corrupt a dead end in the end. Where I had to encounter another trace at the end of the race. Enter uncommon territory, entertain myself with the notion, I was on the move waiting for the corrupt to reenter.

All so I can claim another division to the game. It left me in an entrapment, terrorized by the trace. It had me on the edge forced to hit back with remorse. For the corrupt finalized that ending that took me on journey warning me the troubles were chaotic and I was entitled to an opinion.

Confirming the obvious; I was let down on purpose. It handed me a validation to release that beast. Because I entered a path that hit me at the end of that domain. It was part of a challenge that forced me to remain the same. For I was given a reason to step into a trace that hit me with treason.

One of the reasons why I could not follow upon another reading. Was because I had no trace and the meaning was replaced. I had a challenge to change my attitude; it led me towards a journey that caved in on me. It created a challenge that took me in and forced me to win.

The influence I had created a trauma, that turned into a drama. Where my skill turned out to be a false alarm. It was fake, because I needed to lead, learn a lesson then succeed. It had me break the cycle and feed off the challenge, that handed me a dead end in the end of that trend.

Because I was too busy chasing away the dream, I missed out on a head start. I had to restart and build a new chaotic effect, trapped in the middle of that debt. I hit denial that had me deleting what I thought was the last resort. I had to get back on track and cancel out the impact.

Forced to revive a trial, in the end of that arrival. Led to believe that the trace was too hard to erase. It turned into a nightmare when I reached my peak. I was troubled, torn in more than one direction forced to hit back at every resurrection. For the drama served was a road to recovery.

It remained the same. I entered new era, feeding off the beginning of a new improved journey. Instead of creating a better cause of action; I reached my pinnacle and hit an abreaction. A detection to a challenge. that failed me when I hit that resurrection that had me facing a trick of the trade.

For the deception to that manifestation, was caused by the corrupts destination. I was led to believe that the trace was part of a final case. It had me facing another dilemma, teaching me a lesson at every final tremor. I had to refine catch up and feed off the corrupts method.

So, when I reached the top, the only thought left behind was the one that served me well. So, when I hit the end of that final trace a given response will lead me to believe that every drama failed me was because I was not ready to receive. Just undo what I thought was the last resort.

A release to hand me peace had empowerment me. I had to repeat, reclaim, and follow up on another face. It had me release that feast that forced me to review a troubled mind. It led me to decline and fed off what I had imagined would be my destiny. In fact, I hit a trace that failed me.

I hit the end of that trend, forced to pretend. I was given a chance to hit back in advance and trace that case. It forced me to repeat replace and cover up on a case. I had to refine and follow up on another time. Just to reclaim a diversion to a game that was forced me to press replay.

I was reliving a nightmare and this time around it left me facing another tremor to that dilemma. I had to define follow up on another trace just to cancel out the corrupt and replace that case. Hitting a defect to that rejection, forced me to decline delete delay and follow up on another play.

For my mind body and soul was charged a fee, and my

dignity was being tarnished. For the corrupts final test had me on request. I had no time to repeat that quest, because the challenge was too hard to report. Because I was left hitting the corrupt at every everlasting resort.

I had to follow up on a restoration to that manifestation. It led me to release, rely, and follow upon another contamination to that manifestation. I had to rely on the corrupts method to get by and even then, I was left troubled in the end. A trace part of a case had released a demon to replace.

It forced me to repeat a vision to the mission. A feast to that traced that case and forced me to release that beast. It caused an effect and had me requesting a trend in the end of that trace. It had me replacing a case. While the corrupt ponder, the mission and wonder for a pointless competition.

Presented with a force, I had no choice but to hit back with remorse. The case that had me face another trace was pointless. I was on the edge trapped in the middle of a raid that had me repeat another bad day. Convinced that the energy that passed me took me in and failed me.

It was leading me towards a journey, working towards a line up; of disastrous effect. I had to follow up on a review, feed off the concept, and trap he who knew. It was part of a trace, that faced me just before I hit an encore. I hit back with a challenge that had me questioning their motive.

I had no trust, to regain that game, because I was on the

edge; gambling another bad day. Where the only thing that served me well, from within was the task. It led me towards a journey where I never get in, and the only choice left was the one that hit me from within.

So, when I hit the end of that trend the final trace was becoming. The corrupt were on the edge; waiting for me to pledge. Because I was led to believe a lie, it had me facing another fear to get by. I could not repeat redo nor follow upon another review. Because I was lost for words.

For those who knew were sabotaging my mission right through. I was not to question a thing for the method was too hard to engrave another challenge from within. There were to many interests in my mission I lost my will to win. because I was on the quest of making it happen.

I was given a challenge to reserve the right to hunt the corrupt down and hand them a warning. For that scheme was discerning, it had me second guessing: troubled within. All so I lose my light and live my life with the energy that served me right from the beginning.

All I had to do was enter that review and follow up on another clue. Case closing that feast and repeating another request. So, when I hit the end of that trend the only game left was the one that had me hitting what I thought was the last resort; and the end of that request that had me give in.

I had to fight back, for what was part of a defect, had me

detach. I had to feed off the trace that led me to regain conscious awareness again. Because he who knew, was too busy trying to get through. I was finalizing the method that had failed me from within; haunting me every time I tried to get in.

Winning another inning, was part of a trace that had me forced to hit back and replace the case. So, when I hit the end of the race. The choice I made, was part of a misled act of kindness. For the condition to the mission was part of a follow up on another competition.

I hit an outcome, a warning; where the corrupts method was part of a test. It had me turn the events into a trace, a challenge that had me fast-forward to the next quest. Facing me every time I witnessed a failed test, in the end of that request. It was part of an escape; yearning for deliverance.

Where I was to give in, based on a case; that had me failing another test, from within. At the end of that trend, that forced me to pretend, just to claim, move forward; remain the same. It gave me a chance to follow up on a trace, that had me awakened from a warning that hit me with a yearning.

Even though the trace was never detected with a tradition. It did establish an ending that was pending. I hit the mission facing another competition. It conditioned every violation, that had me returning for another competition. For the energy that faced me, had me returning for yearning.

It gave me a second chance to hit back in advance.

Where I get in and present the corrupt with another trace. It was handing me the conclusion a need to repeat, for every validation to that mission was accompanied by a competition. I get in reap a reward, finalizing the concept.

CHAPTER 4

♦ ♦ ♦

FEEDING OFF MORE THAN I COULD CHEW

I was restoring another plot, giving the corrupt a chance to own up. But the thought became the last resort, hitting me and running will be worth more than the outlet, because I fell into a death threat. It was to bring forth an unexpected event, that had me stagnant to my development.

It was an upcoming event, that led me towards a journey that had me vent. It was part of a trace that had me on the edge, about to repeat, replace and clear the deck. All so I can claim a written report, to a game that had me starting again.

Even though my confidence was low, the energy that had me retrieve; caused an effect. It had me reprieve, trending for a chance, to belt the corrupt in advance. It served me well in the end and the only way out was the way in and even then, I had no freedom to challenge the corrupt from within.

My freedom was cut short and I had no time to return and hit below the belt. For the corrupt were on the move, trapping me at every final recall a fall that served me well and had me rise. Assuming that the trace was embracing a case, every time I was served wrong.

For the trend was way too hard to overcome. It had me prepared for one more outcome. I hit a system overload and the only way I could stand tall, was install a backup. I was to push and shove the corrupt in the corner and finalize that trace, so I can rise above that fall.

I had to erase that trend that had me break the silence in the end. It was caving on the concept tormenting me at every level. As if the trace was part of a case that was trending, it had me forced to hit back with remorse. That is when I knew I hit the end of that curse; that was about to reverse.

It handed me a level of challenges, just so I can catch up and feed off the trace. Terminating the corrupts level of madness and harassment, forced to get in feed off the energy from within. Then when the time come burn the pages. Releasing that demon that forced me to revive another dive.

It had me on the edge leveling another trace to that case that caused the effects. It would lead me to a destination that will hand me a reservation. it would state a fact handing me the evaluation to undo that manifestation. Before I could revolve, revive and follow up on another dive.

I needed to repeat and reclaim, another diversion to the game. Forcing me to repeat and undo that ongoing review was harming he who knew and reaching out to he who had a clue. Where neither of them knew what to do, because I fell was injured and had to go through the healing process.

I was stuck, trapped in the middle of a challenge, that had me sitting in a rough spot. Trying to come to terms with the lie, had created a misunderstanding. It entered my realm added sin; according to the corrupts final win. A passageway that took me out of my comfort zone.

It had me repeating a list of demands. Warning the corrupt they hit a follow up. Forced to return and finalize that ether; that served me heaven on earth. I was taught a lesson that left me to release that feast, it took back where I was started forcing the corrupt to delete delay and finalize that trace.

It led me astray; it had me facing another bad day. I took the initiative and faced another trace, just to open a brand-new case. It had me in the end of that trend provoking the corrupt, by giving in and handing them the trauma from within. It broke the silence, led me to hit back with an alliance.

Handing me the evolution I needed to resolve the issue. Where I was given the all clear and the opportunity to hit back with scrutiny. It handed me a chance to repeat that trend that hit a home run and forced me to release that beast that harmed me in the end of that trend.

Where this time around, it gave me the upper hand to follow up on a brand-new theme. Where I get to retrieve and follow up on a new improved journey. Where the corrupt were well on their way feeding me an establishment not the manifestation. This time around what I planted was granted.

It was a seed that held me up and helped me succeed. It was planted long ago but it was not nurtured properly. It remained in the soil, healthy but it did not grow; according to my needs. For those who knew were on the raider attempting to steal another key.

For the troubles were not as appraised as I assumed the result had me facing the final frontier. It was failing me as time grew and that is when I knew the corrupt were failing too. For what I assumed was part of a commune had me embrace that case and feed off the trend.

It had me break the silence in the end. Left forced to redo, undo, convey, and feed off the corrupts method all the way. Repeating a list of demands was creating an entrance to a journey that had me returning for a yearning. It was taking me for a ride at every initiative and forced to undo a review.

It was my way of getting through and feeding off the corrupt. It was part of my final revue, where every avenue changed my perception. I hit an evolution, just so I can skip them too. I had to continue to grasp at every energy, just to bring forth another trace to that case.

It brought me joy, for he who attempted to harm me, had brought me forward. It created an anomaly, where he who spoke in tongue. He had no freedom to cave in on the system. I was about to fall fail and embark in a path towards a feed. Where every trace had me on the edge.

Then without furthermore, replace another case. Giving me the incantation to break the intention. For the realization I hit an expectation, was enough for me to see the journey was imperishable and the trace undeniable. It was consistent with the end where I get in and follow up on another win.

Where those who form an alliance to get in, and lose their identity. Handing me the win so I can claim another competition. For the game had me feeding off the method, that had me remain vigilant to a test; that was gambling my truth. Handing out a lead to cut the corrupts method.

For that presentation had not given me the right manifestation. It was part of a past test, that I failed to achieve. Because I had to follow up, on a trace that led me towards a journey; replacing every thought given. Giving me the power to feed off the last resort, with the forbidden.

I was taught a lesson it gave me the indication that I hit the end of that pathway. Forcing the corrupt to challenge me all the way. It was part of a trace, that had me hit the end of the race. Where I got in and fed off the drama from within. For every trace had me hit the end of the race.

With one motivation in mind and that the was to storm through. On the condition it harms the corrupt at every manifestation. Where their foundation collapses and they lose concentration. So, when they hit the end of one trace the nest they harvested remains empty.

A trend that will harm their existence in the end, in the meantime; I had to remain patient. Not allow the corrupt to hold me back because I forced my way in and fed off the trace that had me facing another case. Meanwhile I had to continue to reap those rewards that come my way.

Reach my potential, by creating a trace that will serve me well, at the end of the race. All so I can press replay, while I delete and delay. Feeding off the corrupts method all the way, was not part of my goal. I wanted to let it go, set it free, and finalize the outcome so I can continue to grow.

Moving on was not an easy task, I had several on my raider; stirring the pot. I was not to get caught up in a presentation; it had the corrupt manifesting another investigation. For the lead, was towards a journey that brought me forward. It became part of a game, that was gambling my dream away.

It was a challenge that had me in, delaying every win. Pressing replay so I can win another inning, was not part of the game it was a challenge that was returning to drive me insane. I knew something was wrong, I had no choice, I had to get in and the only way to play it; was enter at my own risk.

I knew everything I was handed was too good to be true; but, yet again, there was no exit. Playing it was the only way I could live it. There was an entrance, that did not feel as if I was welcome, it was fake false; it hit me with a pulse. A trace that trapped, and tricked into believing I was succeeding.

It threw me off track, with a challenge that had me reserve for more clues. It changed my views, long enough to catch up and belt he who knew who caught up without my approval. I was fed off by he who decided to return and reclaim his truth. It forced me to undo and prepare me for a clue.

In fact, I was being thrown off track left to embrace the case, kick back and feed off the tremor. What a dilemma, where I was given the all clear. It had me release and break the silence, so when I reached that trend, the only terrorist remained was the one that was alarming me.

Warning me again there was trouble ahead. The only way I could force my way through, was trace trap and challenge the corrupt so I can give in an feed off the trend that broke the silence in the end. It had me reliving a nightmare, a trace that was presenting me with a curse I could not reverse.

It was as if I was locked away in a cryptic affair. I was living in a basement full of Demons and dragons a fairytale that had me reaching my potential with a mystical view. A trend that made me believe I hit a dead end. It was a test, that had me come to terms with the fact; I was an Artist.

My imagination took the best of me; it threw me off track; straight into what I thought was anomaly. Because everyone, I met were negative and toxic they made me think it. Eventually it took the best of me I started to believe it. Once again back in that rut trying to remain strong.

When truly, I was strong all along. Because there were several on my raider, waiting for me to fail. It created a war in my vicinity; I was fighting of those who were stalking me. A lost cause, a troubled journey that led to troubled mind. It had me questioning their method and feeding of the deception.

Handing me redemption added with an evaluation had created an amendment. A forum that served me well and caused an effect, had me trapped in the middle of that defect. All while going through the motions, I was hit with a verse that stalled while was sailing through.

Whatever was to stop me caused an effect handed me the strength to push through. It gave me a chance to reserve the right to undo another clue. A trace that had me prepared for another trend. Where I was given a reason to hit back with treason.

I was returning to follow up on a goal, a reason, that had me competing. I ended up forced to heal from a fall, that led me towards another pathway. A passageway out of the old into the new world praying to God this time around it will lead towards a positive outcome.

On the hope it had left the negative behind; all so I can continue to grind. This time around I let go clear the air, clean up the debts, and undo the threats. Make sure the entrance to that ongoing frail trend, serves me well in the end. For, I hit an encore well deserved and well desired.

I had forced my way in and declared what was mine; in the end. Because I earned it fair and square. It cleared the debt before it became a threat. It gave me the entitlement; I needed to release that beast. It forced me to redo another review. Because I was taught a lesson; just before I entered.

It held me back; where I had to take a step back to get back on track. Because the follow up on another career, became a second guess; toward my quest, on request. It was part of a journey that opened a whole lot of new skills. It led me towards a trace that failed me in the end of the race.

Because the path I was on, was based on a conspiracy that held me back. It was the point, that was useless that took me on that path. It presented with a lifelong goal. It was handing me the resolution I needed to repeat another trend. Feeding off the corrupts method handing me a dead end.

The truth had me replacing a nightmare. I knew what I wanted to do, and what the key had installed for me. It was part of a follow up that was enticing. That decrease created, a pace, with several affairs. An unknown step towards an ending, that gave me a second; chance to release the beast.

It created a test, that will help me progress. Giving me the impression I won the race. It helped me step forward to the right direction. Where I get in and finalize that win; serving me well. It gave me the righteous way in, a method that had me warned; it held me up and failed the corrupt.

For they were the reason why I hit the finals with treason. I was attacked by a competitor that had nothing of importance to offer humanity. Just fake and false friendship with a dead-end love affair that will lead to war in the end. It was part of a heresy and a vicious circle and cycle of events.

Feeding of the trace, led me to relapse. In the end I had nowhere to go, nowhere to turn, I was locked in, praying for a chance to get out of that swing of events. Forced to hit back and feed off the impact. The game became inhumane; handing a reminder, I did this to myself.

Because I was hit, with a presentation that led me towards the wrong destination. I did not give in to the corrupts demands. They were way to harsh; it gave me a second chance to hit back in advance. It had me stepping into the unknown, pretending I had no freedom nor foundation to hit back.

It was part of another manifestation, a presentation from a past event. Where every situation, caved in on me and served me a trace that forced me to get in and feed off the race. It had me on another level a warning the curse, could be reverse if only I could return and face my fear.

It was a challenge to help me face the facts, and hit back while I catch up and restrain myself from losing another game. In the end of that trend, I was facing another fear feeding off the corrupt so I can start again. Facing another presentation, a price winning key; that manifested my destiny.

A journey that brought me in and gave me the win I needed to feed off the trend that handed me the manifestation to break the silence in the end. An energy that had me constantly on the run starting fresh and feeding off the outcome that presented me with a key.

A final contamination to man infestation brought me forward. It was part of an endeavor that turned into a vendetta. It created a piece that forced me to release and uncover that trace that handed me the energy to finalize that trend that served me well in the end.

Several were using me to get in, the thought I was part of a syndicate never failed me. They had me on their raider using me as their final degree, stalking me like no other. They were meant to save me keep me save, but they took their time waiting for me to fail so they can prevail.

I went for an outlook that forced me to release that beast. It had me warned there was no trace to embrace, just a case to cause an effect and feed off the defect. I was taken for a fool; left to return and finalize that impromptu. Forced to redo another review, because I was taken with an abrasion.

I took it all in and was faced with a virtual development. It had me second guessing instead of approaching the deal. Because it all seemed way too surreal, what was going through my head was cut. The opportunity to make something of it was shortened; an unexpected opposite effect

Leaving me sitting in a broken chain, no reaction. It had me waiting for the corrupt to return; push me off the edge. Releasing that demon that forced me to embrace that trace. It caused an effect and gave me the energy that I needed to release that beast. Fail the corrupt at the end of that lease.

For they took me for absolute fool. They initiated a trend, that pushed me off the edge, straight into a ditch. A test of endurance had come and gone. So, when I reached my destiny the only thing that saved me was the energy that forced me to redo. Trap me in the corner and follow up on a review.

All so I never get in, nor preach my truth. If I did, they made sure that I would come out the other end, looking as if I was insane. An insecurity, a no brainer; so, they can look better. A blaze, was lit and the gas lingering around the perimeter; ready to burst in to flames.

What I knew and what I was told to do; was verified in columns, and paragraphs. All I had to do was read between the lines, and follow up on a dream. Make no excuses face a fear, and return for one more hit. Erase that feast that had me repeating another trace; at the end of that dead-end.

CHAPTER 5

♦ ♦ ♦

STEPPING FORWARD STRAIGHT INTO A LOCK DOWN

I was less likely to achieve a goal; for I was stuck trying to prove I was innocent. I was cut wide open, the huge urge, created an extension; that handed me redemption. A warning that had the lead, took me on journey troubled me, with a trace that had me hitting the end of the race.

I word it wrong, fighting the case that had me erase the trace. For those who were wanting the same as I created a war in my peace, they took me in and fed off me from within. It was as if I had to release, extend the warranty just to give the corrupt a chance to belt me in advance.

It had me forced to hit back with remorse. I had to follow up on a trend, that had me repeating a dead-end. It had me on the edge interacting with the demon that forced me to pledge take the role of a drama queen, giving me the energy I needed to repeat and follow up on a trace.

All while I create a war in the corrupts pace; trending every time I had to decline. For it all went belly up and I had to surrender to get back on track, warning me the energy that served me then forced me to repeat the now. Handing me the faith I needed to skip the corrupts method somehow.

So, I decided the next best thing was to return and repeat; when I needed a boost of energy. A warning I had taken it, way too far handed the corrupt a chance to hit back in advance. I was warned of what was to come from that waste; it gave me a second chance to hit back and face that fact.

I was wanting to fight a system that had me feeding off the trace. It led me towards a journey that forced me to release that beast; it had me facing another feast. Wasting valuable time causing effects and trapping those who knew so I can catch up and feed off the corrupt.

For that journey that had me on the go, succeeded only when I hit the end of that trend. All by harming those who face a true reality. I was left to face a terrible lie, a challenge that served me well when heaven hit hell. It took me in; a fed off me from within.

I had to trust the process, for I was left finalizing that leadership. It had me sitting pretty, warned I was way too hard on myself. Where the only way I could return, was repeat sacrifice he who attempted to harm me. All while reach my potential with one more loyal outcome.

A challenge that hit me repeatedly, under the raider; ran its cause. It forced me to release that feast, that had me forfeit. Failing me when I hit the end of that trend, because I had no friends, my family were not to get involved either; because they would be in danger too.

My freedom was cut short, constantly being traumatized from those who were Romanced by the cause. Just so I do not fight back and state a new fact. It caused an effect, left me forced to give in; on a condition I can hit back from within. Feeding off their soul; leaving them suffering Holistically.

It was my way of living on the edge, for the trace become potent. It ended in a faith less likely to release that beast. It had me forced to return and finalize the end. Warning me, the energy that had me cursed was part of a trial an error. A final tremor to hand me the chaos I needed to repeat.

I had to re-appeal kindly state a fact while I get out of that trace that had me erase that case. I had to repel and push the corrupt into hell. Leaving them held back, in that world suffering. While I go back on track, there were several things I needed to overcome to kindly state a fact.

I had to create a better outcome; it was the only way I could stall. I was to release and finalize that beast. Because I was hit with a trend, it held me up and forced me to pretend. It was part of the test where the trace was based on a case, that had me on the edge of becoming diabolical.

For the method was challenging, not only I was stuck hitting back with a rough edge. But the corrupt caused an effect and took me in and fed off me from within. I was torn in more than one direction forced to release that beast that had me facing another ordeal.

A test at the end of that request, caused an effect. It had me regain conscious awareness again. For the corrupt faced me and had me challenging another ordeal. It gave me a second chance to release that feast; it led me towards a journey I could not revive.

All because every journey had me face another case. It was warning me there was no world departed and the free ride derived, from the corrupts finals. A day that was to remain unraveled and the sanctum remained the same. The suffering was no less than the quest.

It had me forced to redo and follow up on another review. There was no foundation to process because the journey that served me was based on the challenges that had me hit a hint of madness. I was taken for a fool, it took me in, and fed me a lie and handed me the reification to get by.

As a result, a leadership to the next manifestation, had become known. It was part of a trend that had me request another final. Where I get in create a trace, request a test, and push the corrupt in the corner so I can restrain and follow up on another game.

Returning for one more theme, had me facing another scheme. I had to catch a break and repeat repel and finalize the indifference that put me through hell. For the corrupt restored my energy took me in fed off the trace and broke the silence from within.

I had to break the cycle, wrap it all up and follow up another trace. It was a dream that ended in tragedy because several wanted to play it but gave me grief while the attempt turned into what I thought was the last resort. For they were attempting to clean me out and hit me doubt.

It fed off me while attempting to embrace another trace to that case. It was causing an effect while handing me doubt. It had me recreate another trial while I stepped into denial. I was fed off from within; there was no case worse than the one that had me on the edge; starting fresh.

It caused an effect; it took me in and led me to believe the challenge was reprieved. For every trace took its toll, I was faced with a germ, violating my world. It had me facing a case that had me fight for my life; just to win another bite. I was given a hint, trapped in the end; with a rude awakening.

It became part of a warning, where the corrupt saw me easy. The decision to face me with a yearning had become interactive. I was led on, taught a lesson left to release that beast that forced me to embrace another case. For they no longer had the power to project or devour.

I had to face another case and then line the corrupt up for another chase. Meanwhile pretend that the curse was part of a verse, For I was given a reason to return for another first. A trace that lined me up for a lead to compete with he who formed an alliance and tried to have me fight back.

Conditioning the mission so I can replace the competition, was unravelling my mission. I had to fight back to get back on track. For every time I was served a challenge the position, I was put in was delayed. I was forced to retrace another case and condition the mission so I can catch up.

I was on the move facing another raid, only to witness I was stuck once again. Trying to pretend with a trend that will lead the corrupt towards a dead end. My way in gave the corrupt a final thrill a challenge that will serve me well when the corrupt hit a final spell.

Where the only thing that come to be, was the energy that was left behind. It was part of a trace, to hand me grief. For the trial and error was to break the cycle and the corrupts unity. Forcing me to hit back with scrutiny. Handing them constant denial, after the fact; so, I grieve over the incur.

It warned me there was no trace, worth the chase. I had to hit a follow up to my favor. Undo a clue create a trace and force myself to repeat another case. I had no freedom to overcome that outcome. I was on the edge trapped in the middle of an ongoing riddle.

When the time come, I could overcome another

outcome. I enlisted that trace and took it in had no freedom or foundation what I had was another investigation. It served me a final I intake. Where I had a chance to undo the clue and follow up on another review.

I had to face my fear and kick start a follow up. I was hit way too many times, by those who knew and wanted to screw me right through. My challenges were way too strong to break the cycle and follow up on another trend in the end. I had way too many hang ups, to recount and ascend.

The decision to let it go was not taken lightly. For I had several who knew, that had their eye on me, as if I was their prize at the end of the tunnel. In fact, I was an upcoming event that had me forced to vent. I was given a trap to overlap, just to release that beast that forced me off the edge of reason.

The corrupt were stalling, kicking a fuss, and handing me a reason to hit back with treason. They were trying to sabotage my journey, attempting to reclaim the game and follow up on a past endeavor. It had me face another dilemma, a lesson that led me to believe a lie.

All so my life can continue to fly by. It had me forced to hit back with remorse. The trauma and fear took over; I had to take an absence of leave. Just to get my head and act together, so I can retrieve whatever was given by those who hit me with a condition that handed me an admission.

A trace to that case, had me canceling another race. It

was part of a past trace, replacing another case. The corrupt were prejudice, it gave me a second chance to break the cycle in advance. I had to face another fear just so those who knew can take the initiative and follow up on another review.

It had me break the trend, feed off the edge of reason. When I hit the end of that repugnance; a service well over done. It did not make sense; for I was left to release a beast. Fight off those who heave at me at every trace. An assumption that handed me a level of disgust.

Where ever move, had me rough, for what reason; only the corrupt knew. I was assuming the worst because the drama took a turn for the better. It was the only truth that will set me free and state a new precedent. Because they were hiding something of importance; I became a victim to it.

It forced me to reclaim and delete delay; follow up on another bad day. For they were torn in more than one direction. Afraid of what was to come from that outcome. I would have trapped that trend that traced me in the end. A given response to a dead end; for those who knew could not pretend.

For those who took me in, shocked the corrupt from within. I owed them nothing, I gave them my all and they decided to work against me. All so I fall and never rise above it all, not only did they open an old wound, but it closed what was to come; just so I can catch up and feed off the outcome.

It ousts them out the door and their plans were too hard

to acclaim. For the decision to break the cycle and start again was warning me. For the only thing that created the trend, started to release a feast that forced me off the edge. It was about to break the silence and the cycle to that arrival.

It had me request a brand-new test; a trace that caused an effect. It broke the silence that had me raise above and beyond. I get in and feed off the urge that harmed me from within. When I fall, I heal and the follow up will seal the deal. A path to power through, endure to feed off the allure.

It was the magnetism, that fed off the speed. It pulled me in and pushed me forward, so I can win. It planted a seed trapped me in the middle; so, I can succeed. It had me return the favor so I can continue to dive and delve into another trace. A drive that took me in and fed off me from within.

I was not entertained nor obtain what I thought will bring forth a reality check. It was not as attentive as it was meant to be. There was no trace or treasure just a curse that will serve me a trial and error. For the assumption became part of my redemption; given the all clear.

It handed me a challenge to hit those who hit me. For the assumption, that the power in numbers will keep them strong and I in suspense. An extension that fed me more than I can chew. Where I needed to repeat repent case close that debt and finalize the mission to hand me a proposition.

It led me towards a validation that had me stringing the corrupt along. It had me trying my luck lining me up for one more chance to lead the pact; all while I continue to succeed. Trapped in the middle of a failed conspiracy. Taught a lesson added with a follow up, on a trace that broke the cycle.

All so I can catch up replace that trend that forced me to pretend. I had to rebel against those who saw me well and wanted to watch go through hell. For those who nurtured me with a trailer of test had me on the edge, ready to repeat and attain another gamble at the end of the game.

I had to release that demon that forced me off the edge; straight into a ditch. It had given me a whole lot drama handing me a thrill, where I caught up and caused an effect. Just to get back on track it had feed off the trace that pushed me off the edge; straight into a curse that held me down.

I was harmed at the end of that verse; it took me down. It led me to strengthen on a case that had me reach the end of the race; it forced to repeat all while I got back on track and pressed delete. So, when I hit the end the only thing that held me up; was the last thing that brought me forward.

Where I was given a trace, that reached its toll. I reached my energy only to witness I was given a failed outcome just so the corrupt can get another crack at it. I was hit with a curse I could reverse and a challenge that took me in and faced me with a trace that served me well from within.

All while I was catching base, I was second guessing, trapped in the middle of a trace. It had me facing another case. It had me hit the last resort forming an alliance so the corrupt can continue to hit back and face me with a new improved trace; saving me at the end of the race.

The corrupt were on the edge, trapping me in the middle trying to pledge was uncanny. It had me switched on ready to repeat rebel against those who follow up on an upcoming spell. For the curse had me rehearse I was about to reverse. For those negative thoughts took over my positive outlook.

I guess I had to come to terms with the fact the corrupt were torn. I was trying to claim my truth, pause effects and trap he who tried to trick me. So, when I hit the end of that road, the only thing that led me to win was the last thing that had me finalizing that energy that served me wrong.

For all it did and for what it was worth, the trace became a trap and I was lost for words. The only thing that came to be, was the last straw and the beginning of a new improved clue. Where the energy that force me to hit back and feed off the trace; handed me the power to undo and devour.

I was to achieve my goals and return the favor. Then acclaim what I thought will bring me forward. Where I was working towards a lead; a fighting chance to face another fact. For that energy that had me facing another trace, in the end of the race; had me breaking the rules and the cycle.

I had to return the favor and present the corrupt with a test. It was to hand me the presentation; a need to process. All while I catch up and face another fear. A case that was pending, was closing to my favor. For the corrupt took it to far, they saw me easy and wanted to please me.

All by attempting to feed of me. Where I had to tread carefully so I can get back on track. I had to face another tactful event. The one I needed to release that feast. For the journey that had me facing another breed, took over and led me to break the cycle that had me on arrival.

I had to release that feast that forced me towards a pathway; handing me an edge. It was creating a trend, that faced me in the end. Leaving me once again wondering; was the corrupts plan worth it. I was seen as an easy target; they were causing effects. It had led me to believe I was the chosen one.

That was half the truth! I was chosen; but the way it was written. It was an opposite reaction to that abreaction to lead me to a destination that had me warned once again. Then again, at the end of that trend, I was to break the silence and make sure the cycle will remain steady and silent.

When the contract was breached, it will lead the corrupt towards a dead end. Handing me the freedom to pretend, protect my soul from reliving a trace. It had failed me and left me hunting for another trial and error. For what I thought was the end of one trend; was the beginning of the end.

CHAPTER 6

◆ ◆ ◆

STEPPING FORWARD WITH FAITH ON MY SIDE

I was handed a chalice of affairs, a prize-winning adventure. Not quite the way I expected it though. It was played out, with a condition of self-doubt. I was taken for ride, grief stricken and left to suffer while the rest prosper. Leaning me towards a break through, where the lie took over the truth.

It turned into a review; that left me case closing another trend in the end. The closure had me free from he who was charming me. I was expecting a challenge that had me free from anomaly it served me droves, it took me on a pathway; that forced me to release the beast.

I was well on my way, creating a better day. The only

way to do so was hit he who hit me. It was the only way I could return and press replay. It tore the corrupt in to shreds and handed me a revolver that will save me when I hit the ends of that trace that forced me to repeat and replace.

Where my spirit took over that trend; having me facing another dead-end. It became a for filling event where my journey took me on a path, that forced me to elite another fight. It created a brand-new sprite. It gave the corrupt a dead end, to that warning, that served them a yearning.

I had to return and foretell a future event. It led me towards a journey where the corrupt had me on the road to recovery. I was hit with a trace that was pending, it had me on the edge surrendering for another challenge that come my way. So, when I reach my pinnacle, I could press replay.

I was left to relit a new flame, a renewed game. The old flame blew out and the new flame was a lie. It was to give me a chance to fight for my life, on the hope when I witness the truth; that will kill me. Not only I knew but trying to keep up with the program and get through was a challenge.

I had to fight back, cause an effect, create a piece, follow up on a new lease. For the truth was not as praised as I thought. I was stuck lifting my spirit on my own, hoping the corrupt will get caught and lose their faith. While I continue to ripen on my own, feeding off the trace and reaching my peak.

Even though I knew that the lie, will eventually come out; so, did the corrupt. Instead of letting it go they kept stalking me. Waiting for me to fail, and never prevail. I had to let go, step into the unknown on my own. The hope I rise above that fall was my highlight.

Feeding off the corrupt so I never lose hope, was a challenge. I had to hit rock bottom again, where this time around reaching my peak had no recollection. I had to reconsider that resurrection. Catching up and facing a fact, gave the corrupt a chance to advance and I change my perception.

It hit me with a constant reminder; he who knew had me locked in; breaking the rules. I was silenced from it all, because I felt the energy change, I was to return with a wound to heal. While I rise above and beyond, trapping he who knew and he who had a clue.

For the troubles that served me well forced me to replace and follow up on another case. I had to curse he who doubted me, just so I can catch up and finalize the interruption that handed me a resurrection. I was given a challenge, that led me to return; failing the corrupts method in turn.

It was handing me the foundation to release all inhibitions. I was stuck trying to get out and fight off a new thought. Handing me the challenges to recreate a trace and force my way in, all so I can condition the mission and replace a forthcoming case. For the corrupt lost their power to erase.

It was part of a passion, to have the corrupt vent

towards my direction. I was too busy trying to repeat that I took the wrong approach. It had me facing another trend in the end, where I had to follow up on one more fear. A challenge that failed me when I hit the end of that trend.

It had me facing a return, an event, testing the patience of those whom fight back. It was part of an evil plan to restore the energy of those who reclaim and follow up on another game. A disunion based on a presentation that had me waiting for the next investigation; to come to fruition.

It was part of a game that had me facing another trace to that case. It caused an effect and presented me with a debt. For I was given an expense, that made me an easy target in the end. A challenge that forced me to hit back and leave me waiting for the energy to release another feast.

It led me towards a journey that created a piece it forced me to interact and break the cycle at the end of that trace that restored my energy and took me in and forced me to catch up and feed off what I thought was the last resort. It was part of a syndicate at the end of that return.

It forced me to release that feast that had me uncover another piece. A troubled event, where the energy that faced me in the end, gave me fake revelation just to reveal and revive another investigation. It was part of a trace that served me well and presented me with a final a restoration.

Where I get in reach my destination and feed off the resurrection. It faced me just before the corrupt were about to form an alliance added with a dispute. It had me reaching the next destination with a revolver where I get in and feed off the trauma that trapped me from within.

It was holding on to a trend that was pending, served well in the end. It had me raised up and trapped in the middle. Where the corrupt were meant to hand me a clue, just to follow up on another review. For what I knew, was enough to release that beast; that served me a new lease.

For I was warned and left to struggle in between, all so those who wait patiently can redeem. It had me harmed, and forced to hit back with a charm. I was left to redeem and follow up on another scheme. It had me righteously on the move, taken for a ride and left to retell another tail.

I was led on left to release that feast, so when I reach my peak, the troubles were weakened and I got a chance to return and release that feast that burst into flames. Handing me the energy I needed to come first. Where the cause and effects, forced me to resurrect; harming me at every finally.

Where I was left to release that feast, it had me recruiting another piece. For those who restored their energy by feeding off mine were about to get a taste of their own filth; because I decline. It gave me the power to undo and devour. Following up on another division reclaiming a competition.

Because every game was a gamble, it forced me to return and fail another theme in between. For I too, had to reveal, a faith less likely to release the beast. It led me towards a challenge, that had me release another feast, burnt in the middle of a final riddle.

It had me waiting for the corrupt to silently erupt. It presented me with a trend that was failing me in the end. For what I thought was the last resort forced me to reclaim, divide, and conquer and remain the same feed off the game. On the edge presenting the corrupt with a new pledge.

I had to undo a scheme that scammed me in-between. It presented the corrupt with a validation where they got in and had a chance to repeat, and trap me in advance. I was in the middle of that case that was causing effects. It stirred the pot; it had me rise from that dead end.

It was part of a trend that forced me to pretend. I had to reveal, revive, and follow up on another dive. It had me requesting another feast, trapping those who release; trying to find peace. A trace that measured the truth had me requesting another lead it handed me a new improved vision.

Just in case I lost my place, for every trace had me facing a case. Where time did not stand a chance, to stand still, for the made-up story in my head; kept me balanced and ready to face the day ahead. An anomaly that served me well then, left me unwrapping a reservation; to that manifestation.

Where I get in, feed off the win and entrap that debt; that had me fast forward to the next threat. For I was on the mission to reclaim another competition. Revealing what I thought was the last resort. For what it was worth the trace was based on a case that had me returning for another verse.

I did not give in, nor did I give up, I gave it my best shot. It failed the corrupt, so I can catch up and feed off the trace that led me to release that beast. It forced me to redo reclaim and follow up on another gain; once again. Where I gave in and the challenges that served me well.

Where the only troubles that served me well forced its way in. It was the one thing that had me cursed, serving me a tunnel and a turf of failed events. Where fighting back will hand me the debt and the threat to feed off the trace that led me towards a journey that forced me to replace.

It faced me with a trace that hit me at the end of the race. So, when I hit that trace, I get to break the cycle feed of the lead with denial. I was lied to; it gave me a second chance to provide the corrupt with a final glance. Where several gestures caused an effect; handing me a defect.

For what they had done left me undone. Trapped in the middle of a long-term effect, for what I knew threw me off track and took the method and handed me a truth the one I needed to break the cycle and the corrupts silence. For what I called a lead to the next threat was a debt paid off.

It had me feeling the trace, trapping me in the end of the race. Where the thread was cut and the only thing that served me well from within was the trend that broke the silence. Where it had me restoring my energy daily. Before the corrupt had a chance to hit back in advance.

Where I had to follow up on a journey, a threat that ended in tragedy. I had to tread carefully; forced to hit back with remorse. For the plot backfired and I was back on track escaping another vision to my mission. Hitting back with unity a follow up to a past trace; a case I can replace.

I was led to repeat and rebel against those who put me through hell. Stirring the pot every time I was handed a challenge. It left me branded, forced to release and follow up on another feast. If I did not trace it the way it was written I would be stuck living a lie.

Stepping into the unknown was the only way to get by. Where justice took its toll and the only way I could redo another review was follow up on one more clue. Just to give the corrupt a chance to get by. For the challenges that had me refrain myself also took me and fed off me from within.

For what was to come, had me facing a trace, with an outcome that had me reserved for another service. I was given a reason to hit back with treason. I had to chase that case that caused an effect and forced me to resurrect. For what I knew, what was to come; had me overstimulated.

It gave me a second chance to hit back in advance. For

the trace was part of a case that took me in and fed off me from within. It had me on the move warned of what was to come from that outcome. It was part of a challenge that gave me the edge. It had me on the move waiting to be served.

It gave me a second chance to restore my energy; feed off the corrupt in advance. A given reason to break the cycle and hint to whomever. For the trace was based on a case that led me to believe the energy that served me well. Handing me a challenge to release that feast; forcing me through hell.

It was too hard to break, the cycle, because the challenge that took me threw me out. I was lead on lied to, trapped in a world that served me wrong. It caused an effect and had me lead the pact just to get back on track. It had me on the edge forced to pledge, just to rise above that tide.

I was to believe in the lie, as if the if it was true. Then hold on to it for life, so I fail every trial; where every trace had me hit a case. It stirred the pot and gave them a chance to rise above it all. While I rot, with the fact that I had made a difference. No one wanted to except the fact I did contribute.

The trust became a case I had to erase, just to follow up on a vision. It caved in on the concept stirred the pot. It took me on a journey that forced me to redo and follow up on another clue. A wager was created around my space hoping they could repeat redo and fail me right through.

A follow up on a review became apparent, for the

corrupt seemed to have taken me for a fool. I had found peace, but at what cost, only I knew. For the journey that forced me to renew, failed me right through. It caused an effect handing me a defect, led me towards a journey of restoring my energy.

It forced to release the beast, then when the time come overcome another outcome. It had me hitting back where the corrupt saw me easy. They forced me off the edge, trapped me in the middle and served me wonders while I caught up and broke the silence.

For every time they returned and forced me to decline it had me dive in and follow on a whim. If I made any sort of comment, I would be tested, teased, and left for dead. It had me stepping into the unknown with a gutsy move. Where the trace became a case and the trend belted me in the end.

The reason why the corrupt got in, was because they cheated. They were entering my realm holding on to me as if I was their enemy. I had no freedom, only foundation a key to change my destiny. It handed me the end of that trend that served me a warning. Helping me get out of that doubt.

Where eventually I was handed a trace that will trouble me. Forcing the corrupt to hit back with a final lead. It had me living with my needs forcing my way through lining myself up with denial. Where I had to catch up face another trace, lean towards a new development.

A clue to clean up the mess and break the cycle. Leaving

those who knew hunting for clues reasoning with the stage where I get in and upstage the corrupts method so I can get in and speed up the process that served me well; while being forced through hell.

All while I watch the corrupt confess, deter, and finalize that experience with a trace. Where I test the corrupts patience and finalize the edge of reason with an expense that hand me accomplish another trace to that case that was causing effects.

I need to compete compel and follow up on another upcoming spell. It had me feeding of the trend, concocting a challenge that changed my turn of events. It turned my revelation into a final investigation. It was part of a trace that was pending and a trend that was never-ending.

It taught me a lesson; it forced me to alleviate another curse to that verse. The corrupt were not invited, the invasion to my privacy had been consummated. They entered my realm without my permission, creating tension at every competition. I had to redeem and follow up on a new theme.

Just so I can catch up and clean up the mess, and face another test. I had to get back on track and request a brand-new condensed test. It was to help me follow up and lead me to a destination where I break the cycle; handing the corrupt denial. As I release, undoing every forthcoming piece.

I had to remind myself there was no threat, just a challenge. It had me face another trace it caused an effect and trapped me right before I hit another encore. It was part of a test to serve me well and present me with an upcoming spell. I had to release that feast that forced me to reload.

Warning me once again I had to acclaim another version to that game. It had me feeding off the past. Releasing that demon that had me forced to hit back with remorse. I had to reclaim another division to the game diverting the corrupts method all the same.

A trend that lined me up for a dead-end, had me forced to pretend. I was left to repeat and follow up on another trace at the end of the race. Then when the time come repeat another outcome. Forcing the corrupt to undo that dead end that handed me a death threat.

Where every trace had me focused on what I thought will work well for me. In fact, it was part of a trace that led me towards a journey that threw me out of place. So, when I reach my peak, I am back fighting for my life. Releasing that demon, that forced me to fight back; breaking the cycle.

I was pushed off track, where I was to replace, stir the pot and follow up on another plot. It handed me the evaluation I needed to repeat reclaim and follow up on another game. It had harmed me facing an anomaly; trying to fight off an old theme. A flame that had been burning in-between

For what I thought was the end of that terror. In fact, it was the beginning of another. Where I was fighting for my life double time, expecting a miracle again. The only thing I was given from it all, was a physical ailment where I fall and left me frail. All that was left was the last recall; that had me stall.

CHAPTER 7

◆ ◆ ◆

THE DRAMA ADDED WITH TRAUMA IS NOW IDLED

For the attempt to make difference, in my world had become a challenge. I was not aware that everyone I met were fighting for the same key. I was being belted by several who knew and decided to reclaim another division to the game. Assuming belting me, will harm me completely.

For they thought invading in my privacy, will serve them well. It will fail me and put me through hell. I had to free myself from that curse that forced the corrupt to return and hit me with a verse. It had me facing a fact, forced to react. Pray to God I come out the other end free from that dead end.

It was part of a fake and false act, where kindness only existed when the corrupt persisted. It had me on the edge of requesting another vision to my mission This time around whatever happens I do not lose a thing. The energy that forced me in, faced me from within and forced me to win.

I had to continue my journey, breaking the silence. Feed off the greed and pretend that every challenge was on the mend. The energy that had surrounded me, pushed me to redo, follow up on a review. It was creating a war in my peace; forcing the corrupt to renter and press release.

It was part of a pointless affair, where the corrupt were waiting patiently for a chance to advance. By pushing me in the corner and handing me the conclusion I needed to release that beast. It forced me to embrace a kind way in; just to erase another bad day.

I needed to rectify that wrong move, handing me the choice to serve me well and fail me at the end of that upcoming spell. It forced me to pretend, then have me return for another dead end. I was reaping a reward, that forced me to hit back and follow up on another cord.

A case that had me on the edge of reason, had me reading between the lines. It had me facing thew end of that test causing the wrong effects. Because that will to break the chain had me on the other end starting again. It gave me a chance to face my fear and fight back.

It was handing the corrupt a curse they cannot reverse.

A trace they could not rehearse, because I hit the end of that presentation undoing every investigation. Hinting to the corrupt they had no chance in hell of replacing that case. Because it was that trace that served me well.

It handed me the energy to incur and put them through hell. All while I get in and present the corrupt with an extension; just to teach them a lesson. It had me repeating what I thought would be the last meeting. It was the beginning of an ending that was pending.

Handing me the entertainment to release that beast; forced me to find peace. It took over the truth and I was taught a lesson that made me see, it was not my lesson; it was not meant for me. I took it that trend and traced it in the end. For that reason, it led me to believe that the trace was retrieved.

It was part of a case that forced me through hell. Releasing the last thing that had me facing an informal win. I was to resist, persist, undo a review. What did I do to deserve a final reservation to that recognition. Where I was taken from my comfort zone, towards another arrangement.

I had been on the same journey, for so long I lost my will to live. The trace became; unbearable I was led on trying to remain strong. Every time I tried to repair something, I was stuck with no help. The decision to pull the string had me forced to get in. Finalizing that edge that broke the silence.

Even if I reached out for help those who sustained, chose to remain the same. It forced me to hit back with ongoing stigma. Putting them in their place, was the only way I could remain positive through the whole ordeal. It was restoring my energy take it in, repeat the event, and call it a win.

They were causing effects, damaging my spirit so I never resurrect. So, I decided to venture out on my own, test the waters and pray to God I get through. For those who knew were dead to me. I was seen as an easy Target, belting me from within to get in was the only way to accept defeat.

I found opportunity to reap a reward, where I trapped the corrupt to get ahead. They were raiding my head and assaulting me in my peripheral vision; an absolute outrage. Every time I had to refine I was given a reason to hit back with treason. All so I never see a positive outlook ahead.

I was on the move returning for a yearning. For the turn of events that had scheming for another scene. It had me on the edge a total pledge to remind myself I could not create a better win. Because my understanding was not part of the trend, it was failing me consciously in the end.

I hit a deception that served me redemption. For the next path was releasing a feast, forcing me off the edge; straight into a ditch. Undeniably heart-wrenching case, that had me on the other end waiting to be served. For the corrupt were invading my privacy, hitting me with a curse.

Forced me to reverse, write a wrong passageway. So,

when the corrupt reenter they cannot press replay. For the right to undo, fight back with a clue was my way of accepting an end of that final burn. It had me facing another fear, straight into a challenge that had me waiting to be heard.

No feast to release, no final to find peace. Just a challenge to undo what I thought was the last resort. For the next deception, had me releasing another final. It forced me to undo replace and follow up on another case. I was led on and let down, for way to long; forced to hit back from within.

For what the corrupt thought, and what they achieved from that forethought. Transported me, back on track. It brought back a memory, of a situation that opened a door to a destination. Where I survived a nasty fall a hit where the resurrection was worse than the deception

Giving me the power to release the beast, had me fight back. I had to make sure the next time the corrupt return for another hit it will bring me forth. It will have me feed off the trace, that served me well. Presenting me with a curse that will challenge the corrupts method.

Handing them hell on Earth. Where he who knew will no longer cave on the concept. Nor will he have the power to reinstate me with one more listing. Because I was torn, left to be on my own facing another trace to that case. It had me cancel every vision that caved in on the mission.

A task that brought me peace had me release. I had to lead the pact, once again; while I suffer in silence. For the drama was too hard to bear, for I was stuck trying to skip it all. Waiting for the performance to unfold and I return for one more chance to revolve.

I had to reclaim my truth force my way in so I do not lose my way. All while trying to catch a break every step of the way. It had me breaching a contract, waiting for the right time to release a feast. It had me cause an effect; trap he who knew. Forcing me to repeat, rebel; against he who had a clue.

In the end the debt became a threat. I was taught a lesson, left to lead the pact. It had me reconsider what I thought was the last resort. In fact, it caused an effect pushed me of the edge and repeated the same game. All so I can claim another division to that mission; that had me refrained.

I was on the edge trapped again trying to release that beast. It forced me to return for one more chance to hit back in advance. I was left to rely on he who knew to get by for he who had a clue was waiting for me to undo that ongoing review. Where every time I stepped forward; I fell into a trance.

I was hitting a dead end in advance, recreating a second chance. Just so I can catch up and fast-forward to the next task. It was way too easy I had to fight back feed off the trace create a better outcome and redo what I thought was part of an everlasting trend; the last resort to that dead end.

Just so I can catch up and finalize the ending that was pending. I was about to lose my soul, feed off the trauma that had me rise above that fall. Finalize the edge with one more key, hitting common ground. I had to review cause an effect where it hunting me down will create a crown.

It had forced its way in and led me to win, handing me a clue where the result had me finalize it all. A chance to rise above that terrible fall, had me again fighting for my health. It was leading me to a destination where every choice handed me a confirmation.

For what I knew was half the truth, the other half was still pending. That is when I knew the corrupt were about to give in and surrender their win. Because it was a joke, I had to evoke and follow up on another key. A challenge that will serve me well; ending the corrupts tradition.

For what was to come from that outcome was not part of the trace. It had me on the edge questioning every case. Not only I was led on but it had me create an ending that was pending trying to avoid it had me on the hunt hitting back with the same old trivial game.

It had me in the loop lined up for another haunt. It was creating a heavy load, for every time I was haunted by the past the present became avail. I become second best to that trace that had me sail through. The only way to let it go was go through it all heal; then follow up on the next road.

Where I get in, fail on one thing, sail by and allowed me to repeat replace and feed off the edge, that had me on the go it had me pledging for another key to get by. It was part of a follow up on another ride of a life time. Just so I can give in and release that beast that was harmonized from within.

I had to play it live set a light and finalize the energy that served me right. I had to rise above and beyond the occasion; where every test created peace. Where it stated a fact, just to get back on track. The given key, was based on a case; that forced me to release the beast.

Feeding off the trace, forced me to repeat and replace. Was undeniably out of my control. I had no validation nor the earning to hit back with a theme. The scheme in-between changed and I had no freedom to remain the same. It became an expense that was unworthy.

Because I was stalling, I was forced hit back; remorseful. The only thing that gave me the power to win, was the trend that had me favoring the corrupt in the end. It was part of a final, a dedication, indicating that the commitment that served me then; led me on.

I was holding back a trace, that was trending. It was part of a lesson, that forced me to return and hit back. Determined to fight back whatever was haunting me then handing me the power to review and follow up on a case that had me replacing that one thing that hit me and fed off me from within.

when I reviving another survival technique, my method caused an effect and released that demon that pushed me off the edge. It had me on the urge, stepping forward replacing another key. All while I get back on track and feed off the energy that was feeding off me.

I had finalized that pact with an impact, losing my patience after the fact. I was trying to catch up, catch a break and cause an effect that will hand the corrupt a dead end in the end. Now that I hit an ending that was pending, my method forced me to hit back. I took the initiative and face the facts.

Resurrecting from a cover up, that had me returning for a yearning. Led me towards a presentation that warned me, I hit the end of that investigation. It had me feeding off the impact, creating a trace that was heaving at me when I entered freely. Apparently, I was not humble enough.

For that reason, I was not welcome. It was part of a trace that had me replaced. It was based on a key note, that was meant to release the beast. But all it did was follow up on another feast. A trace that served me a curse, I could reverse. I did not see the energy unfold; unless I gave in.

The only good thing that come from that win, was the trace. It served me well; it opened a door to upcoming spell. For an investigation to that finally restored my energy.

It had me forced to hit back with remorse. In the end of that reservation, it forced me to replace a curse; I could not reverse. I was on the edge, recreating a trend that had me waiting patiently to release that demon in the end. It was part of a trace, to cancel out the case.

It had me fast forward to the next gift, a presentation that will lead me towards a new road. A feast that will humble me at the end of that lease. So, when I got caught up, I could replace that trend that had me returning for a dead end. The good thing was the energy that surrounded me did not fail me.

It took me on a presentation, that had me reclaiming another informal investigation. An indication I will fail and lose my thoughts had come and gone. I did not give in, nor give the corrupt a chance to win. I was Troubled by the loss that I had when I fell into the deep.

Because the trace was part of a case that took me in and fed off me from within. I was left to present the corrupt with a failed window to opportunity. I was not nurtured and it left me recoiling and unraveling a creation that stirred the pot a challenge that was interval to that interest.

It had me invading in the corrupts final delusion. A trace that handed me the end of that trend. It revolutionized the task, where the truth was giving me the power to undo and devour. The fact I was on my path, trapped me in the middle of a deception that handed me redemption; causing an effect.

I was troubled, waiting for the trace to unfold. It had me facing another tremor. Warning me, the only thing that come from that win, was the trap. It had led me to release that demon from within. It had me forced to catch up, just before I hit an encore, an energy that took me in; and fed off me.

All so I lose my identity, never get back on track. Losing my way through, was not the way to go though. I had to follow up on a day to get justice. I lost my freedom, about to lose my foundation if I fought it. I went too far, after the fact, hit hard at the end of that train of thought just to get back.

I had to follow up on a dispute, cancel out the corrupts method. Then when the time come keep up with the program. There was too much pressure no fun intended. I was taught a lesson left to hit back with an entity that pushed me off track. I had to build a new foundation around the old.

What I had to do to go through the motions; was terrible. I had to top it off with task and refrain from the energy that led me to believe the worst; too hard to embrace. The track was not an easy task. I was left encourage myself, to move forward, feeling discouraged; for no one motivated me.

Fear that I fell into a psychosis that was created by he who knew. It was his way of locking me in. Increasing my energy to give me the strength to fight back. It forced me to let go and follow up on another show. presenting the with a challenge that will hand me praise and leave them astray.

It did not make any sense, for the corrupt were way out of line. It was my time for me burn and instead of getting in, I was forced to undo return for another review. I had to undo and feed off he who forced me to repeat another damn key. Reclaim and present the corrupt with a dead end.

I hit the end of my tither, and at the end of that trend. I was handed a demon disguising himself as a friend. It left me branded, trapped with the thought that I was rejected. Just to hand the corrupt a chance to return and steal another key. What a warning that had me yearning for another scheme.

I could not state a fact, nor even create a better trace, to get back on track. Because everything I did made me see the truth. I hit the end of that trend that had me breaking the silence. It had fed off the case that lined me up for a dead end. A trial and error that served me a terror.

What I had to do to create such a cold heart, was not as easy as I assumed. Because I was left to hit the corrupt with a trace, it had me repeating and reporting my every yearning. For those who knew, were too busy trying their luck to hand me bad luck. I on the other end fighting for love.

What they were attempting to achieve; had me heave. It handed me a chance to hand them my resignation; so, I can continue to go with the flow. Feeding off the trace that me at the end of the race. It was part of a harmful debt; that led me towards a traumatic event.

What followed will no longer project itself, for it taught me a lesson. It was a presentation, that handed me out a forethought. It was part of a trend, that had me returning and reuniting with an old friend. An enemy that had me facing another dead end.

CHAPTER 8

◆ ◆ ◆

WHEN THE CORRUPT CONTINUE TO PLAY THE FOOL

While the corrupt were playing the fool and broke every rule. I was on the other end trying to find peace. Trapped in the middle of a trace, that had me fast-forward at the end of the race. I was facing another warning and the only way out was the way in; even then, I had no freedom to win.

I was to repeat and correct a past tradition, a prediction that gave the corrupt a chance to hit back with a partition. It had me reliving a minor competition a dramatic effect that had the corrupt reenforce another debt. It was part of a dead end, that was creating havoc in my vicinity.

I was to repeat what I thought was part of a good cause. In fact, it was the opposite effect. It left me trapped in the middle of that debt. I was taught a lesson, left to depreciate the trace, so when the end come to be. The entrance to a new journey, will trap those who sat in my world unwelcome.

It was to create a cause an effect, a challenge that will help me resurrect. I had to face that trace, that had me case closing another trend in the end. Because I was given a trial and it became an error, I fell into a trap that caused an effect the terrorized me at the end of that debt.

I was given a reason to break free from that treason. For that feast warned me I was nowhere near that lead. Forced to break the cycle with remorse, then follow up on an accomplishment. Where I was to get in, feed off the trace that hooked me up. Faced with a case that had me forced to replace.

I was left in a world where the trace had me on the other end; facing a conspiracy. I was taught a lesson taken for a ride and left to pretend while the rest follow up on a new trend. I had to go for one more key, ignore the corrupt and face a final return hitting back while I get back on track.

It was a trace that took me on a path that had me undo another review. It was part of an easy task; forced repeat, replace; start again. I had to feed off the challenges that forced me to drive the corrupt off the edge. In fact, it was part of a trace that had me replace the old with the new.

Where I had to make do with that wrong move. It forced me to release that beast that had me reclaim another feast. For that trend had faced me in the end of that trace. It had me break the silence and breath again. Where every time I was given a clue the corrupt saw me easy.

They started to release what I thought was the last resort, in fact it was part of a final release to hand me the injustice, I needed so I can find peace. A follow up on a good deal that forced me to reclaim another competition to the game.

It was the corrupts way of creating a competition, that had me reliving another mission. A nightmare in-between. Where both competitors were to give in and hand me a new review. Where I am forced to give in and follow up on another improved impromptu.

It was part of a lineup that gave me a follow up. It had me on the other end returning for anew clue. It was part of a given, I get in and feed off the competition. So, when I reach my peak, I could review, follow up on a brand-new skill. A journey that had me on the run, scheming for a better outcome.

I was waiting patiently, on the go so wanting to make; so, what happen. I was judged trapped, left to erase another case. Forced to overcome and out do an overview. An outlay that had me overstay my welcome. Just so the corrupt can continue to steal another vision.

Assuming they had the power to make do with another prediction. Where my revision, became a competition It had me feed off the vision. Where my decision to hit back with the same invasion restored my energy, handing me an expense and the exposure to hand the corrupt an indecency.

There was no power no freedom nor even a prediction that handed me peace. The foundation that, became part of a predicted spell served me well. It took me on a journey that forced me to reclaim and recreate a competition to that mission. It had me face another case, cause an effect.

It gave me the power to undo and devour. It was part of a good deed, where every challenge haunted me. The desire that I needed to release that feast, forced me to overcome and outdo another review. For I had undone to many knots, it led me to a pathway; forced me towards heresy.

In the end the freedom that restored my energy took me in. It faced me with another trace it caused an effect and presented me with a defect. A well-deserved outcome that had me on the run caused an effect it warned me; once again. I was about to descend from that resurrection in the end.

A trace that had me hold on to the upcoming event. Led me towards a destination that caused an effect. Presenting me with a brand-new threat. I had no choice but to hide, way too many on the rise. Every chance they saw me. They found opportunity to chant; belting me with same game.

Hiding in my own world, did me no justice. It handed me a conclusion, that served the corrupt a chance, to return and hit me; within my vicinity. A place where I was to feel safe was being invaded it left feeling uneased. Praying to God to save me and harm those who were invading my privacy.

I had to run and hide, that was the only way I could return and hit back with a karmic effect. leaving me fearing the outcome caved in on me because my prediction was the corrupt break. I was not interested, for they were aroused by the chase but they ignored the outcome.

Because the assumption took over the redemption. I made no sound it gave them passion and the energy to return for another trend that was pending in the end. It forced to undo and pretend that journey was part of the living dead. For the corrupt saw me as an easy target.

It hit me with a violation, assuming that will bring them luck. In the end it was all a bluff. Just to scare me and roughen me up. In fact, it stirred the pot, forced me to undo a cover up and a review. Just so the corrupt can face me again and repeat a trace to that trend that overrated my head.

I had to release, all inhibitions, then repeat that entrance to that competition. It forced me to release what I thought was the last piece of the puzzle. A task that brought forward an everlasting conquest to that trend failed the corrupt in the end. Face a trace, all while I finalize that case.

It forced me, once again; cornered by he who harmed me. A charm, that had me requesting another test. For harming my spirit became a part of a conspiracy that had me face another informative event. It had many preoccupied in a mission wanting to return and recreate another competition.

A quest to that trace forced me to replace another forthcoming case. Because I had to pretend that the trace was part of a final case it caused an effect and forced me to redo while I follow up on another review. For I was given a chance to hit back in advance.

Every trace faced me with the notion, I hit an end, with the right to break the curse. It had me come first. A trace at the end of the race became apparent. I was left with the notion I hit the end of that method. Recreating a clue that forced me to reenter review and follow up on another exposé.

A story plot that had me forced to hit back with remorse. It took me on a journey that had me remain vigilant. All while the rest were harmed by the conquest; hitting back on request. Where that devotion, demolished the corrupts final frontier. A second chance to fail a royal trace, to that case.

It had caused an effect and presented me with a defect. It forced me to redo and disclaim a division; to a game that was handing me a review. Where every informal investigation had me facing what I thought was the last resort. I hit a thought that faced me just before I was handed an encore.

It was part of a case that caused an effect and presented me with a challenge that led me to believe that every journey was a burden. In fact, it was a breakthrough, it opened my eyes and forced me to rise. Handing me a conclusion that served me well when I hit that upcoming spell.

I was impacted by the energy that had me forced to hit back. Based on a case that hit me at the end of the race. It was purely to cause an effect and break the silence. Forced to hit back with remorse. It brought me to my knees, stepping into a trace where I needed to face a major fall; rise above it all.

A drama worse off than before. Leaving the corrupt anxious no more. A wanting to return for more was handing me a chance to hit back in advance. It was Leading me towards a journey that served me well in the end of that upcoming spell. A fault of my own accord, because I gave in to early.

It became apparent to me, that I jumped and swam to early; into a swamp. That is when I knew I was forced to hit back with a rebellious chase; a challenge that cannot be replaced. Because I gave in when the time come, I had no choice, had to rejoice and follow up on another outcome.

For what was to come, had me forced to hit back with remorse. I was stuck trying to hit back following up on a trend that served me well in the end. Where I get to do my own thing and pray to God from within that I remain safe. For what I was tempted to do was only because I was torn.

It taught me to fight back with a trend that had me facing another dead end. A silent test that had me hit back with a request, from that bad omen. Because it had me forced to reprieve. For the challenge that served me well then, failed me now. It became a dead end that forced me to induce.

It was part of a rejection, that had me forced to come forth. I was taught a lesson and left to hit back with remorse. The challenges that come my way were part of a heresy. It had me face another case presenting me with a verse that will help me reverse; while the corrupt come first.

It was to belt the corrupt at the end of that cause and effect. It served me a trace that failed me at the end of that trend. for I was led on, leading the blind, trying to remain sturdy while the rest were attacking me. It had me face another trace trying my hardest to erase.

Leaving it to chance, just because I was let down, had me facing another bad day. I had nowhere to turn and the only thing left was to regain and recall to the game. I was to begin a new win. A challenge that will have me face me and hand me another trend in the end.

Harming he who had the curse reversed, forcing me to come first. It was part of a trace that trapped me and the only way to follow up on another attack was recreate a challenge to help me get back on track. It had become part of a song and dance, that forced me to hit back with remorse.

The troubles that had me case close that trend, led me believe I was starting again. In fact, I was right on track, trapped in the middle of a track-record. A past offence that had me reach my potential hit back and start again. Fighting off that demon led me to believe the worst was the curse.

The energy that forced me to press replay come my way. It had me working towards a challenge that served me well. it caved in on the concept and gave me a chance to entertain my spirit in advance. I remained silent, vigilant to a game that caused an effect; it brought me forward nevertheless.

I went through the energy that broke the silence. It had me work towards a journey, that had me repeat and start again. I was burnt with no recognition, fighting for my life at every repetition. The lesson lived were forced. It had me remain silent it gave me another chance to hit back in advance.

It was part of a trend that had me break the silence in the end. Because that trace became unbreakable and the trend become part of a survival technique. It led me towards a journey that had me return for one more turn. It was meant to be part of a key that had me face another case.

I had to delete delay and follow up on another game. A challenge that took its toll, it had me face another chase forcing me to repeat. I had to replace a curse, then verse he who helped me come first. A play that served me well and put me through hell, pushed me in the corner.

It gave me a second chance, to release that demon. I was taken on an adventure to advance my knowledge. It was to methodically forced my way through, to the next level. Feeding off the end of that trend that had me face another dead-end. It had me lose my balance and fall in to the deep.

It was a death trap, that warned me I was nowhere near that cluster. It was a challenge that had me look further. As if I was stuck and the drama took over the rough the recall and the trend that had me follow up on another dead end. For what was about happen kept me silent.

I had a list of things to do, but the list of demands had convinced me otherwise. It was overcrowding my skills and the energy that had me torn. The call back had become a huge success. I had stalkers stirring the pot staring at me as if I owed them security. Where everywhere I went tried their luck.

It forced me to repeat by handing me bad luck. I was trying to recreate a recall to that faith that had me stirring the pot. But all it did was give the corrupt another chance to hit me in advance presenting with another chance for me to return the threefold.

It had me releasing that demon that pushed me off the edge; straight into a ditch. I turned over a new leaf, page after page torn burnt so I can start again. It gave me a chance to rewrite the script, only to witness I was torn at every direction for that reason.

So, when I reached that peak I was forced to repeat. It was causing an effect, breaking the silence, and trapping the corrupt at every turn of event. Holding up all while holding on was not part of the beat of the drum. For every entrance became a vengeance.

Forced to hit back with a yearning. A follow up that served me a key, it had me forced to hit back with remorse. Facing another warning, was a challenge it caused an effect and presented me with a key. It had me reach my limits without fighting back; I reached the end earlier, than expected.

It was part of a trend that forced me to pretend. It had me facing another dead end. I was left to repeat, haunted by the trace that had me incur another final stir. It had me feed of the energy that had me reserved for another threat. All while I resurrect release that beast and cave in on the idea.

It broke the silence that had me warned, that the only thing that led me on, was the trace. and trauma that faced me had favored the corrupt. I was given a reason to rely on the corrupt for no reason. So, when I hit the end of that tragedy, it will hand me travesty to continue my mission.

Where the only thing that come to be was the energy that served me well after I was put through hell. Because I caught them in the act of attempting to harm me again. It created a presentation that had the corrupt release that final feast. It caused an effect that released the beast.

I was given a reason to hit back; little did I know he who knew was about to harm me right through. I hit an ending that had me pending and a trail that restored the energy of those whom were on the mark of skipping it all. Just so I never reach my potential. I was on the road of recovery.

While the corrupt were on the road of covering up another wrong. I was not aware I was seen as an easy target pushed in the corner right before I was about to make it happen. So, when I reached my peak. I was given a reason to hit back with treason; troubling the corrupt for no reason.

I was on my path, off the edge; straight in to a ditch. Wrapping it up with one more vision. Feeding off that stinge, that cast a spell, it had me wrapped around a trace that served me a common ground and handed me the influence to try my luck and feed off the corrupt at evert trough.

It had me refined, making my mark. I had to follow up on a trace that left me accompanied with a vision. I had to give in, just to catch up and feed off the trend that had me releasing a dead end. It had me out and about chasing a pipe dream, where in the end it came true.

I had all the tools, the freedom was mine, the foundation was fine. I became finicky trying to remain alive. I was challenged with so much hurt; several were on my case trying to break the cycle. My self-esteem took its toll I gave in; I could not see the positive; because no one wanted to see me win.

It had me fail while I grasp for air; trying to reach my peak again. For the corrupt used me to get in, feeding off the trace. It had me weigh down the truth, handing me a dead end to that end of that trend. I was tied up trying to get out and left to suffer without self-doubt.

CHAPTER 9

◆ ◆ ◆

A FAILED ATTEMPT THAT MADE ME RESENTFULL

I was encouraged to do the wrong thing; I had no choice. The corrupt caused an effect, hit me from within. Wasting my time, trying to overcome another failed outcome. I was quickly taught me a valuable lesson, hounded by the past living in the present. Leading a foolish game; fooling myself.

For I was given a reason to hit back with treason. Led to believe that every game was part of a final. Where my train of thought took me in and fed off me from within. It brought forward where every challenge had me create a better outcome. For time did not stand, nor was it set in stone.

I on my own, lined up for a feast, it had me retrace a curse I could reverse. Certain I was entering an agreement. A presentation that shook me at every destination. I had to embrace, follow up on a case keep up with the program. Free myself from a journey, that had me return for one more turn.

A chance to come to terms with the fact the trace was not as humble as I assumed. All because the corrupt were too busy trying to consume. All while I kindly state a fact, look within and feed off the trend that had me whining for answers from within.

I without doubt was having a hard time of enduring, for I was entering a pathway of self-doubt. I needed reassurance at every occasion. Because those who knew were pushing me off the raider where I lost the motivation to return for one more confirmation.

For what I thought was part of the last resort, ended up giving me the ending that was pending. For I too was to extend, then express what I knew because every trace had me forced to replace. It created a journey that had me return for a follow up to that test, that had me request a final feast.

A challenge that had me refine, took me on a path the led me towards the divine. All while I catch up and feed off the trend that led me towards a journey that had me hit a dead-end. I had to cope and question every slope, while I took it all in. Just to see the corrupt win another inning

Keen that the affair of the heart will remain strong. I

was taught a lesson left to repeat and remain violent. All so I can catch up and force my way in, handing the corrupt a chance to win. As I continued to soldier on, in the mist of all. As I was hit with a trend that forced me to pretend.

While I caught on, given a trace to sustain another case. It forced me to replace what I thought will hand me a clue. Creating a trial an error and a foundation that will break the cycle leaving me haunted by the past living in the present and trying to make do with the new

It had me at the other end of that trend, forced to redo reclaim and follow up on another game. I could not revive, retreat, or even create a reality kick. Because I had to replace, redo even follow up on another review. It had me retreat trace and fall in between the crack s that served me a test.

In the end of that request, it had me locked in, booked for another win. Returning to rewind back time, was a move; whether it was wrong or right no one really knew. Because I let it go, set a boundary; that caved in on me. I fell into a trap, that had me forced to press re-play.

Because it was written a certain way. I was left to back up, back down and force my way through. Kindly state another fact. It was part of a game that had me refreshing the old, the new and the constant reminder, I was taught the same lesson; with the same game! Who knew!

It was part of an act of kindness. It gave me a second chance to release, and find peace. I was let down taught a lesson and left to release that beast. Before I fell into a task that had put me through heaven then back to hell. Feeding off the concept, that gave me energy; to release the beast.

I had no trust, in anyone at this point. I had to rely on whomever, to find peace. Even then whatever I did, did not make a difference. For whomever knew, was unreliable untraceable too. He worked in unison with he who had a clue at the time. Leaving me bamboozled with a task, that was masked.

They still wanted me to pay for whatever was concocted in their head; at that time. Leaving me stepping forward locked in fighting for my life trying to keep balanced while the corrupt were pushing me off the edge straight into a ditch. Forcing me to release that feast that haunted me.

In the end of that trend, it created a challenge, where I get in with a fresh start. For what I did to deserve such a serve, took me on a roller coaster. I had to ride it towards a destination where I get in and recreate a failure to the corrupts manifestation. Leaving them hunting one another down.

All while I continue to release and find peace. It was part of a challenge that brought me peace. It caused an effect and trapped me in the middle of that defect. I was misled treated like an alchemist. I was used and abused, just to hand me bad news. A constant reminder I had no freedom.

My foundation had a knot, cracks in every corner. It left

me forced to hit back with remorse. I was given a dead end to that mission, that took me on a pathway of a destruction. In case that cause and effect reached its potential; I was convinced to convey and hit back with an encore.

I had to carry a burden worse than I could imagine. Just to come to terms with the fact the trace was part of a tactful event. It had me reach my potential once over, then return for another dive into the deep. I was trying to catch up; cancel out the corrupt. Where every momentum took me for granted.

A failure to adjudicate was my way of handing them a bad day. I had a permission slip to report all undo the old start new and create a diversion to push the corrupt off the edge. Trapping there existing with persistence. Handing me a faith less likely to follow up on.

For I was given a reason to reclaim another existence to my mission. it created a dead end to the corrupts final threat. A challenge that had me remorseful at the end of that bet. In fact, the trap became a curse, that taught me a lesson. I was to let go force, my way through; without locking it in.

For I was thrown off track, forced to repeat, rebel, and trap the corrupt in hell. All while I test the patience, of those who knew and took a review; following up on another clue. Where I get in and feed off the trend, that had me request a follow up in the end.

Because I felt, I could not reach my peak sooner. I was

left behind, stuck in time warp, trying to make do with that final overview. I had to return with the same yearning. Forced to hit back with remorse trying my luck to hit back with the energy that pushed me off track.

I was put on a path, ready to be replaced. It had me force to hit back, all while I carry on to the next case. It was part of a trace, keen to make a difference. Only to witness the corrupt were on my case, trapping me in the middle of the race. It was forcing me to replace that curse, so I can come first.

It had me on the go. Ready to follow up and go with the flow. I was on the other end, ready and willing to reveal another trace at the end of the race. It was part of a key, that trapped me in-between leaving me wondering what did I do to deserve such a review.

I had no freedom to release nor report, for I fell into a trap. It had me release that demon that forced me off track. I had to rebel against the corrupts thoughts. Fast-forward to the last resort and then hold that key that served me when I hit the end of that trend; that lined me up for a dead end.

For my journey was cut short. It had me facing another warning, the key that I earned and worked hard to achieve; was stolen. I was stuck chasing he who stole it from me. It caused an effect trapped me in the corner and lead me to release that trace that failed me at the end of the race.

Where I had to catch up and finalize that overview.

Feeding off the trace that had me returning for another trend in the end. I was heaving at every corner facing another bad day. Hitting a warning that led me to believe that every trace; had me breathe out fire.

I had to force my way through; it led me to recreate a trend that failed me immensely in the end. All while I continue to catch up pretend while I uncover up another turn of events. I had to undo and follow up on another review. Just to give the corrupt a chance to override; that stagnant affair.

It had me repeating, another truth and creating a dare. Where the corrupt were torn at every yearning. It had me facing another trace serving me a case that had me rewarded at every trend. Because I was led on and left to release that beast. It had me facing another trend in the end.

I was way off to scared to heave, because I took it all in and fell and fed off that win. It had me facing another dead-end. It had me on the edge accepting and undertaking from a thought that hit me when I hit the last resort. The game was part of that everlasting will, it had me hunting for good will.

Haunted by the past living in the present. Trying to come to terms with a cause an effect; a troubled debt. It had me facing another threat. So, when I reach that test, I will return for one more thing a trace that had me trapped in the middle of that everlasting key; a trend that forced me to pretend.

I had to fight the process, request, another test. All

because I was forced to repeat rebel and feed off that trace that put me through hell. It had me on the edge. It trapped in the middle of a threat that had me led to believe there was no trace. Because the troubles were part of a past case.

It gave me a second chance, to hit back in advance. Restoring the energy, that had me releasing that beast. It forced me to undo and find peace; it had me face a debt. Returning for one thing an ungrateful challenge from within. It was to break the silence and feed off the clue.

Where I had to face another threat a challenge that handed the red thread of redemption. For the trace was pending and the case was torn it had me reaching a trend that was broken leading me to a dead end in the end. It had me feeding off what I thought was the last resort.

It was just the beginning of an end, that had me create a trace that had me start again. A task that become a test, that was pending for way too long. I felt trapped, let down even found myself hitting an expense, that had me rise above and beyond that trend.

Warning me the journey had just hit a hold up; creating an encounter with an enigma. An immense tensed trip down memory lane that immersed, into a turn of events. It had me facing another curse returning for one more verse. I had to cause an effect a finalize that debt; forcing me to walk away.

No longer was I to give in, nor follow up on a pause. Because I was left to repeat the old, start new and feed off the concept that brought me forward. I had to remain silent, haunted by the game, hit back at every trial and error. For that train of thought had me facing a terrible act.

For the corrupt were way off, the stalking became an energy that sent me a list of demand. It had me facing another trace to that case. It caused an effect and presented me with a defect. Packing up and leading the blind all while I case close and face another fear to that spear.

It had me stirring the pot, case closing another trace, because that method forced me to replace. It had me stepping beyond what I thought was part of a rejection that redeemed every final recall. A redemption that served me a deception handing me a resurrection to that final preservation.

In fact, it was a service well done and a trace that had me replacing another test to that request. It handed the corrupt another debt. Where I was stuck with a threat, forced to hit back with no regret. I was hit back with violent attack it had me reach my pinnacle then when the time again.

It reserves me the right to hit back and feed off the impact. I was served well; it gave me a second chance to delve into my passageway. Writing a wrong and feeding off the trend that had me regain conscious awareness again. It was advising the corrupt they hit a friend a dead end; a huge expense.

It had me facing another case in advance. It warned me I was given a challenge that handed me a dream that served me well in between. Leaving me forced to break the silence, so I can get back on track. facing another trace at the end of line up that was trapping the corrupt.

For every time I was forced to hit back with remorse. The trial the error and the test that had me reach my pinnacle with terror led me on. It forced me to remain strong and gave me the ending that was pending and the urge to write a wrong. All while I shut the door to the concept.

Leaving the corrupt to remain stagnant to that development. It was part of a strength that handed me the road to recovery. I no longer wish to carry burden that will hand me the gift that will serve me a rise to the occasion. Because the method was based on a case that held me up.

It brought me forward hitting the corrupt with a release; handing me peace. It presented me with a curse that cannot be reversed. I passed that trend that hit me furiously in the end. For those who knew were invading my privacy. On the assumption it will hand them a clear way to redemption.

The scene had changed and I was way too upset to claim another guessing game. For what I thought was the last resort, had me face another trace. It had me return for one more turn, it gave me a warning that served me well. It had me stall long enough to put the corrupt through hell.

It created a train of thought, a follow up to the last resort. So, I decided to let go, feed off the cause and effect. Prepare myself for a trial an error a trace, handing me a tremor. For it had me return with a no show, because I was shocked. Even though I knew the truth for some reason; I was still hooked.

I took it hard, because once again, I was trying to pretend that the end will be my word. I will be able to prevent the corrupt from returning and hitting me with a dead end. A free ride to follow up on another trace, a terrible warning that will serve me well when I hit the end of that trend.

Haunted with an upcoming spell; a challenge that had me stand my ground. Where I had to learn the hard truth; conned into believing a lie; all so the corrupt can win every fight. Where I get by without being harmed, forcing the corrupt to return and follow up on another return.

It was as if I was being blackmailed. The only way out, was to return hit back with a hold up. For he who knew, wanted to use me to get through; sold me out. For he knew what to do because he saw me coming. To he who took a challenge, decided to belt me on a continuous basis.

Just so the corrupt can continue to release, clean me out and find peace. All so he who had a clue can continue to release that beast; that forced me off the edge. Heaving at me at every trace, as if the loyalty card was handed to, he who had me forced to hit back with remorse.

I was straight forward, energized by the truth; served a key. It gave the corrupt a chance to hit back with a conspiracy. I was wrong to believe that the lie will serve me well. It forced me to hand the corrupt a chance to develop and go through what I thought was the last resort.

It was the beginning of a new era, a challenge that served me well. It presented me with an ongoing spell. It had me off with the fairies, where the edge of reason hit me with treason; straight into a ditch. It caused an effect, and taught me a lesson. It led me to release that feast.

It forced me to replace a case. Assuming causing an effect will bring me forth, what I thought was the last resort. It was a key, that had me led to believe that the lie will eventually become true. It will lead the pact and release the beast that force me off the edge; so, the corrupt can pledge.

I had to be patient, either way; for I was on my way. Whatever journey I chose I still ended up where was I meant to be straight into a narrative affair. It served me well and forced me through hell, I raised the buck and followed up on another trend. Leading the corrupt towards a dead end.

Leaving them staring at a wall, with graffiti symbols; that will hypnotize their simple minds. It will break the silence and help me rise above that fall. Restoring my energy feeding off the siren, that was creating an expense that had me warned I hit a dead end.

Waiting patiently for the worst to blow over, all so I can start again. Return, release peace, and fast forward to the next feast. I was to force my way in, cause an effect; so, justice win. Leaving me convinced I hit a dead end, a journey that forced the corrupt to fail; at every trend.

CHAPTER 10

♦ ♦ ♦

TIME TO RELEASE THE TASK AT HAND TO FIND PEACE

A mindboggling experience, was a challenge. It took me on a path, that led me to rise above and beyond. Repeating what I knew; while I was following up on another review. It had served its purpose, for I was well ending the race perse. A final voyage where every challenge; had me void.

I was handed precision, delaying every competition. Because the corrupt had an opportunity to raid my head and feed me danger that forced me to let go and feed off the no show. It served me a stagnant affair that had me lose my faith. It led me towards a task, that fast-forwarded.

I was working on a journey, that turned inward. Leading me to a destination, that caused the effect. A task I so needed to resurrect. It created a trap, that had me face another trace. Giving me the energy I needed to get back on track and feed off the trace; that forced the corrupt out of place.

All so I can get back on track, trapping the corrupt so I can fight back. Creating a better impact. For what thought was pretentious, ended up having me step into a journey that took a turn keen-sighted. It served me well; it gave me the opportunity to put the corrupt through hell.

The pretentious event, forced me to repeat and rebel. It put a hold on me and my destiny; I was jinxed beyond remission. Released into the wild with a challenge that forced me off the edge; straight into denial. I was led to believe every journey I was handed; was not a competition.

It had become a compilation where my destination was bombarded. It was part of a trace, that hit me and haunted me when I fell into the wrong. It had me facing another competition an assumption that had me facing another vision. I was taught lesson while being led to the right direction.

I was pushed off the edge, facing a line up, pledge. It was trapping those who warned me off. It had me cross many unmercenary paths, alongside those who override. Where the only thing that served me well from within; was the holy trinity. Even though my troubles were nowhere near the end.

I had to wallow in self-pity, trace another trend. Where that trial and error forced me to pretend. It had me case closing another force. Just to hit the corrupt back with remorse. It was the only way I could enter and break the silence. While I enter another project towards an informal event.

The one thing that broke me emotionally, also mended my heart spiritually. It led me towards a journey that served me unity. It caused an effect, as I resurrected towards a final test. It had me facing a journey that lined me up for a curse. For I had no chance in hell of returning for a verse.

So, when I canceled the corrupt out, it would lead me to towards the light. No longer living in self-doubt, nor in a lie, where the finals were to create a better trait for those who hate. For I found a loop hole, it was to block those who were using me to get through.

For everyday had me facing another bad day. if I was not careful; I would pay for that too. Where I got in and fed off the corrupts trace from within. A method that was leading me towards a trial an error and a key that had me forced to hit back with a tremor.

It became part of an age gap, an expectation, that brought me forward. Because every generation kept trying new things. I was on the other end delivering the truth. This generation had their own views, and their ideals were according to the method, that was outdated; it became an outrage.

Several were looking for answers, others were following a trend. Some were so confused; they got used, led the followers towards a journey of bad news. I on the other hand, had to look from with to find peace. I could not connect with any generation; everyone I met, chose the wrong destination.

For those who were aware, were attacking the trend; leaving me reliving a nightmare again. In fact, it was part of an expectation, to bring forth a civil generation. Then again, society can view, state a fact, entertain who ever to get through. It is easy to follow a trend so you can blend with society too.

It was part of a habitual motivation, a propaganda to corrupts destination. Things can lead to a huge number of good deeds, then feed you well and turn you into a bad seed. Where you can get attached to a challenge, that may either break you, or cheat on your cycle of events.

Leaving you suffering in silence, if you lose that trend. Stirring the pot and starting again, finalizing that method that pushed you off the bend; straight into a dead end. To break that cycle, will become detrimental event; if you do not tread carefully. You would be fighting for your life, trying to get out.

A frightful thriving trend, that will tease a tedious tie; about to break the cycle. In the end you are left lied to, led to believe, that every dream was part of an event. Having you feed off that trace that led you to face another dead-end. Leaving you chasing a faith less likely to remain the same.

Because I was pushed in the corner trapped by, he who forced his way in. Silently taking me for a fool, failing me just to see those results undo. As if you had no energy to repeat, reclaim nor even see the game come to be. Because the journey was served with an insufficient priority.

My light was taken; it left me facing another trace. An ending to that curse that served me an identification crisis. Forced to hit back creating a trace, that will push me off track straight into a journey; that served me a high society. The one that caused an effect and broke the debt.

It handed me a threat, that led me to survive, a praise to that daze. I had to revive, all while I consciously took a dive. It had failed me at every damn dead end. It led me to focus on another thread of demands. It did my head in trying to get in. Because the corrupt saw me winning

Where every time I faced my fear, the trace became a treasure. The corrupt served me a priority purely because they saw me as a threat. Because I was led on, I had to remain strong. All so I can belt them every time I was hit with a crime. Then delay, delete, elite and proceed to the next fight.

It was chasing a trend that only made sense, towards a final feast. Where the atmosphere, alone can blend with the trend and create a bad omen. If not tread carefully, I could find myself on the edge. Trying to get out of another threat. Hitting a dead end, forced to get back on track and pretend.

I was taught a lesson, with little knowledge, what I did to deserve such a serve. It had me engaging in another final vendetta. There was something in the air, in the mist of all evil for that trend had me forced to embrace that trace. Teaching me a valuable lesson that had me trace that case.

It forced me to replace, what I thought was unconditional. In fact, it was part of a curse that served me well, it became a safety net that put me through hell. All because the corrupt did not cover their tracks well. All they did was get away with what they did at the time of that forthcoming spell.

Giving me an opportunity to return for scrutiny. Leading me towards a journey that had me pay for their crime. In the end the truth will come out and justice will be served. Handing me the end of a well-deserved and desired contest. A trace that will hand me the end of the track record again.

I was troubling the corrupts method, jinxing their kind heart. It had them reminiscing a past event, forcing me to repeat replay and vent. Handing me the curse I am about to rehearse, was covering up another trace to that case. It had me return for one more key, a challenge that will serve me well.

All while I go through hell, for I found my way through, trapping the corrupts method. Giving me the opportunity for justice because the corrupt saw me easy. Just to give them a taste of their own filth. A challenge that had me finalizing truth, hitting the corrupt every time I fell in the deep.

All so I do not lose what I thought I will gain, because every game was the same. It was part of a theme that had me scheming in-between. Before I knew it, I could not follow up on another sham because the game became part of a scheme that belted me in between.

I had no clue, where I was heading all, I knew I hit the corrupt with a beheading. I was given a challenge that had me return and face another trace. I was handed a chance to word it my way. For what I thought was the last resort. Had become the entrance, I was hit at the end of that trend.

Terrified, I would have to start again, where the trace had me replace another case. I hit an ending that had been pending for some time. I was trapped in the middle of a journey, that served me a crime. It was part of a case that stated a fact, it had me picking up where I left off.

A second trial that had me living in denial. A drill that landed me a role and gave me a skill. All while getting back on track pretending that every journey was pending. I had to face another fear, force my way in, lead the pact, and create a dead end in the end of that trend.

It forced me to portray and start again. I had to repeat, establish a new trace, all by feeding off the energy that had me replace. It was causing an effect that faced me at the end of that trend. I was taken for a fool, forced to return and redo another review; just survive another free ride.

Where I get in and feed off the trace that served me well from within. It created a challenge that put me through hell. For he who knew had me create a trace that served me well. I was given a reason to hit back with treason. Righteous as I was it forced me to file for a divine purpose.

Where my consciousness reached its highest and my potential rose above and beyond. It became part of development, that served me an expense that taught me a lesson. Feeding off the corrupts progression. Making sure that every flaw had me cause an effect and close that door completely.

It had me stepping into the unknown, forcing my spirit to outgrow another follow up. Just to release that beast that had me face another feast. I had to remind myself every trial had an error and every reception chased me and led me to believe the only thing left was the energy that faced me.

In the end of that trace, I was given a reason to break the cycle and feed of that division. It had me survive another case, for a trip down memory lane had me fail and I was to lose another trial. Where every trace had me stepping into the unknown creating an atmosphere that forced me to hit back.

For every lesson I was taught, had me refrain from another game. It was part of a brand-new clue, creating a brand-new review. For each season, had me in the loop trying my hardest to bury the hatchet. I was taught a lesson, where every trace brought me back; to where the curse reversed.

It became a clean way out; it had me on the edge; doubting every trace. For whatever reason, I was served a well desired service, it had me refine refill and follow up on another skill. For that trace that handed me the outcome that forced me out of place. It had me facing a disturbed alliance.

Where the corrupt disguised that method, and saw me as an easy target. Where I had to finalize that key. Trapping those who were charming me, all while the corrupt trapped me in the end of that trend. I had to extend follow up on another trend. Where I was given a reason to break the cycle.

For every time I reached my potential, I hit the end and created a piece. A prize-winning section to that redemption that forced me to rise above that competition. A trace to break every violation had me on the run. It was creating an expense that served me well at the end of that trend.

It was handing me a destination to that next reservation. I had to observe the right to fight back at every reservation. Forced to return at every follow up. Then reserve a serve, Where I get a release and feed off that demon that forced me to find peace.

The desire that I once had, was a given, just so I can catch up and feed off the forbidden. Where the end of that trace, had me return and follow up on another case. For what I thought was the last resort. had become part of a lead; it had me foresee, another future event.

For what I knew and what the corrupt thought was true; was part of a second trial. It was to lead me onwards, towards a force that had me hit back with denial. All because I got back on track and faced another fact. A challenge that had me reach my peak, getting back on track.

Where I get in and state another fact. What I deserved was not part of the serve, it was part of a treason that handed me a forthcoming reason. I had to belt the corrupt with one more moral to that final competition. Before I hit the end of that conviction to that mission.

It became part of that forthcoming spell. Where the only thing that come my way, was the energy that served me well along the way. It was allowing me to break the system while I peaked. Feed off the trace, that forced me to encounter and embrace another case.

It had me face a forthcoming spell, so when hell froze over, I could get in return the favor. I was to put the corrupt through a challenge, that will bring peace; to my royal bliss. All while I break the rules, haunting those who form an alliance. Assuming the game they play, was a plan that will stick.

Their plan will restore and I will follow up on a game; play once more. For whatever energy they lost during the that war, it will help them reach their potential once more. In fact, it had me on the edge waiting for that creep to return, for one more chance to hit back in advance.

It was part of a trace that will hand me a case, causing an effect and creating a deception so I can resurrect. All while I rise above and beyond that redemption. A come back, that will hand me the entertainment I need to break the cycle and succeed.

I had to stand clear, release the beast forced to find peace. It had me feeding off the trace, that broke the silence at the end of the race. It had me guessing wrong, forced to remain strong, so when the trace blew over, I could return remain alert and follow up on another incur.

The challenge took me on path that had me reap every reward. It had me finalize the trend that forced me to repent and then have me face a dead end. I had to follow up on a bend, release that demon and start again. For where I was meant to be and how it ended, became final.

It was part of catastrophe to that colony. Trapped in the middle of a trace, that served me well at the end of the race. So, when I caught up, I could undo and follow up on another review. I was taught a lesson just to get through. Before my life turned into a variety, a follow up; from old to new.

Stuck trying to catch up, it gave me a second chance to follow up on a train of thought a past trace that had me face another invasion to that creative trend that served me well in the end of trace that took me on a journey that had me repeat another trail to that survival technique.

Where I was faced with an exemption, to that redemption. It led me towards a final resurrection, a challenge that saw me through. It was part of a curse, that will reverse and force me to come first. It was an expense that had me release that feast. Led me towards a journey, that had me find peace.

A trace that had me reminiscing a past event had returned. It hit back and made me vent, face the end of the race. Return for one more trace then when the time come feed off the terrible act of kindness in the long run. It was creating a trap that led me to erase that final curse.

A challenge where I was to come first, follow up on a key trace those who forced me to keep up. It was becoming part of a key that had me fast forward to the next final degree. It had me feeding off the trace, that led me to respace. Repeat delete, deny the corrupt access; so, I can meet my quota.

It was part of a trait, that had become a forthcoming test. A case that led me to a destination that forced me to reserve, leading me on. It was handing me the energy to face a troubled trend in the end. Then come out the other end trapping the corrupt. All so I can restart that concept again.

I was handed a rough edge, to that hint of madness; causing the wrong effects. I was handed a rumor that forced me off the edge. Where the result was to lead me towards road to clarity; handing the corrupt calamity. A tragedy that will bring me harmony; for grievance took over their peace.

Returning the favor was the only way I could hit back and press replay. A given chance to break the corrupts cycle in advance. No loyalty card necessary, just a final reveal, before I hit the end of that hint. A trace that had me confess another test and follow up on a request.

It was part of a trial an error and doubtful dilemma, where I get in and feed off the corrupt from within. It had me on the go forced to hit back with a no show. So, when I reached my pinnacle, I could embrace that case, that had me facing another informative investigation.

I was in it, too little too late, for the trace had me facing a trend, where I got in about to be replaced in the end. I was taught a lesson, led to believe a lie forced to repeat repel and feed off the challenges that put me through hell. I hit a trace, just in the nick of time.

Where I got in, freely, preparing myself for another window to opportunity. If anything, I paid for that crime and every challenge that come my way had become a trend that forced me to portray another bad day. In the end of that dead end. It was serving me well, trapping me inadvertently.

While I carried on to the next long shot, where every trace had me facing a final. In the end of that sentimental foundation, I was given a reason to look back and finalize the end of that trend that forced me off track where I got to repeat and rebel against those who served me a wrong doing.

For whatever happened, I was given a reason to hit back with treason. Trapping he who had me forced to hit back with remorse. For whatever was to come from that outcome the only thing that come my way was the energy that forced me to press replay.

It handed me concord of events. It had me directing the corrupt towards a destination where I get to feed off that manifestation. It served me a world of troubles. I was well on my way trying to regain conciousness, all while I press replay. Only to witness the trace was part of a case.

It led me to believe I had no freedom to reprieve. Just a wind up, that handed me a hold up. It had me reach my potential way too late. All because the corrupt, kept hitting me running; handing me a run for my money. It had me step into the unknown, warned of what was to come; from that roam.

It was part of a trend, that served me well in the end of the race. So, when things got out of hand it served me a disloyal event of affairs, to break the corrupts cycle. So, they give in and stop attempting to harm my spirit from within. Handing me a second trial for me to reach my pinnacle.

With every denial, I hit a second trial. It forced me to repeat, replace, and follow up on another key. What was to come from that outcome, had me stepping into what I thought will bring me forth. A presentation that was to hand me an investigation. Facing me at the end of that destination.

For he who knew caused an effect, led me towards a journey that had me release. For what I thought was the beast, who trapped me in the mist. In fact, part of a prior affair, that took place in a world that had me replaced. An expense that had me step into the unknown unworthy.

A warning, that had me worried of the outcome, became part of the experience. Where every trace handed me a key, it led me towards a journey that served me well. For those who knew were stalking me, they took me in assuming attacking me with persistence will turn back time.

Working to cover up another sin, from within will hand them resistance. As if them repeating, and cheating will break my spirit. It had faced me with a curse I could not reverse, for every time they saw me rise above and beyond, they would push me in the corner and follow up on another hit.

I had to resist come back to reality and follow up on my peace.

ABOUT THE AUTHOR

Panagiota Makaronis

I have a Master's degree Philosophy and Theology at ACU Australian Catholic University. I also have a diploma in Clinical Hypnotherapy at Sterling Institute and The Australian Academy of Hypnosis.

My studies included Psychology, Neurolinguistic Programming, Meditation and Spirituality. Over the years I have worked with many clients where I delved in Mediumship Clairvoyancy Astrology Numerology Reiki and Crystal Healing.
You name it I studied it.

I also studied the Key of Solomon that was a path I will never forget, learning that method gave me a path on Heaven on Earth! What can I say, that was an interesting concept.

I was on a mission of oppression, to study the human mind and see in hindsight what makes people in society click.

I was so interested about Anthropology and Sociology, I had a lot questions unanswered, so I decided to follow a path of the unknown to see how I can make sense of my reality.

My clients were, experimental to me I was on a mission to investigate the human nature and I met a lot of interesting people along the way.

Because I was quite accurate in my craft, I had several who became quite defensive and could not wait to cover up their mess by challenging me, because they assumed I had a knowing and they could delete and delay me.

That made my life quite interesting it helped me with my writing. I had adventures where I could sense I was on a path of defending my honour while others were hiding behind the truth. Lucky for me I felt that I was being protected by my spirit along the way the Guidance from within never lead me astray.

I had to take an absence of leave, because of family

commitments, I went on a Sabbatical, decided go back to university get my degree, clear my path and bring myself back to reality.

I was fighting a lost cause living another person's life, where it led me towards a destination where I could no longer lie to myself.

During my absence of leave I went on a path of journalism and freelance writing to, I have my own blog on Face book where I write inspirational pieces. Basically, to warn those who are inspired by the truth to set it all free and believe.

Not only in yourself, but in life, because life is to short, not follow others or worry what others think neither. In the end you have to live within yourself. Face your fears and trust your instincts. Because no one really knows what is around the corner.

No one knows unless you stick to the plan and even then, your world can collapse, and you have to start again. I should know! I have had passed several paths, where my foundation was not strong enough to hold me, and it would collapse where I would have to rebuild again.

What a catastrophe!

Having said that, time does not stand still, time is of essence. Based how much can you achieve in one life time just to leave a Legacy Behind.

I strongly believe you must follow your path and how it might look to others it should not matter as long as you can accept who you are then anything is possible.

Where in the end I believe the right presentation will lead you to the right destination if you persevere.

THE THEATRICAL MELODIA OF MY LIFE CHRONICLE 1

The Melody of my life is my Odyssey, an Epistemology; a series of books, short stories based on my Spiritual Journey, and personal development. A method created through my travels founded on my truth, knowledge, and belief system. It got me through the hardest times,

A Sinful Act Of Kindness From The Heart : Chronicle 24

A Sinful Act of Kindness from the Heart; Chronicle 24. A continuation to my memoir; The Theatrical Melodia of my Life. Where one day at a time took a wrong turn, a least expected accident turned my life upside down. An unexpected nightmare. Exiting my comfort zone and hit with another dead end.

BOOKS BY THIS AUTHOR

A Byway Chariot Awaits An Awakening Contingency: Chronicle 23

A Byway Chariot Awaits, an Awakening Contingency; Chronicle 23. A continuation of The Theatrical Melodia of my Life; Chronicle 1. My Epistemology Theory, an Odyssey; My Bible! I swear by it! Where I fell into a trap and a trace that became part of a worrisome outcome.

The Infinite Gnostic Theism Of Evolution: Chronicle X

The infinite Gnostic Theism of Evolution Chronicle X is the continuation of my series of novella. Based on my spiritual Journey and how I perceive the world. An Autobiography and Epistemology. A memoir to advance, strengthen my wisdom and forward my knowledge, for the purpose of survival

Tetelestai Debt Paid In Full: Chronicle Xx

Tetelestai Debt Paid in Full Chronicle XX; It is the continuation of The Theatrical Melodia of my life Chronicle 1. It is a one woman Comedy Show & I am the Comedian. I am to push forth, and preach my critical analysis. A tell-tale story, to catch up, and catch the corrupt red handed

Agrius A Rise Above The Antichrist Chronicle Xxi Is The Continuation To Theatrical Melodia Of My Life. I Was On A Pathway, Towards A Presentation, To Lead Me To The Next Destination; Only To Hit A Hol

Agrius A Rise Above the Antichrist Chronicle XXI is the continuation to Theatrical Melodia of My Life. I was on a pathway, towards a presentation, to lead me to the next destination; only to hit a hold up. An obstacle come my way; a pending trap. I remained repentant, just to get back on track.

The Adventures Of Ari, Stinky, Smelly & Sniffy;: A Legacy Is Born A Search For The Black Onyx Stone

A Search for the Black Onyx Stone; It's Halloween, Ari is snuggled up at home with his mummy Betty, his three teddy bears Stinky, Smelly, and Sniffy, his playful kitten Uri, and his loyal puppy Pouey. While looking through an old box of photos, Ari uncovers stories from long ago of his Greek grandparents, Yia-Yia Dimitra and Papou Costa, who came to Australia on a ship called the Patris, chasing dreams of a better life.

www.ingramcontent.com/pod-product-compliance
Lightning Source LLC
Chambersburg PA
CBHW050828160426
43192CB00010B/1946